Rod Stewart

THE VISUAL DOCUMENTARY BY JOHN GRAY

DEDICATED TO...

"THE CRITICS, THE CYNICS WHO NEVER UNDERSTOOD IT.
WHERE ARE THEY NOW?" (ROD STEWART, 'ONLY A BOY', 1981)

© 1992 Omnibus Press
(A Division of Book Sales Limited)

Edited by Chris Charlesworth
Cover designed by 4i Limited
Book designed by Alun Evans. 4i Limited
Picture research by John Gray & David Brolan

ISBN: 0.7119.2906.8
Order No: OP 46762

Picture credits:
Front cover: Rex Features; back cover:
Redferns (1964), LFI (1974 & 1991); Richard
E. Aaron/Starfile: 43b, 59t&b, 66l; John
Bellissimo/Retna: 67t; Dominick
Conde/Starfile: 82; Lydia Criss/Starfile: 56b,
79; Steve Granitz/Retna: 81b, 88t; Hulton
Picture Library: 4; Larry Kaplan/Starfile: 60t;
John Lee/Starfile: 45l; London Features
International: 8t, 17, 22, 23, 25, 26b, 29b, 31,
34, 35, 39t, 43t, 46, 48t, 49, 51, 54t, 55, 56t,
60b, 67b, 69t, 70, 73t, 74t, 75, 78, 81t, 86t&b,
89t; Janet Macoska/Retna: 41t; Paul
Natkin/Starfile: 68, 69b; Pictorial Press: 8b, 11,
12l&r, 20, 21, 27t, 28r, 44b; Barry Plummer:
27b, 30, 32t, 33t, 38t, 40t&b, 41b, 54b,
57t&b, 58t, 63, 73b; Chuck Pulin/Starfile: 1;
Michael Putland/Retna: 28bl, 32b, 33c, 50;
Redferns: 9, 26t, 29c, 33b, 38c&b, 39b, 44t,
45r, 62; Relay: 28tl, 29r, 37l&r, 47, 48c&b,
65, 72; Rex Features: 18, 19, 36, 53, 58b, 61,
64b, 66r, 71, 74b, 77r, 85t, 88b, 90, 91b; Bob
Scott/Starfile: 80b; Gene Shaw/Starfile: 83;
Vinni Zuffanti/Starfile: 64t.

Exclusive distributors:
Book Sales Limited,
8/9 Frith Street,
London W1V 5TZ, UK.

Music Sales Corporation,
225 Park Avenue South,
New York, NY 10003, USA.

Music Sales Pty Ltd,
120 Rothschild Avenue,
Rosebery, NSW 2018, Australia.

To the Music Trade only:
Music Sales Limited,
8/9 Frith Street,
London W1V 5TZ, UK.

Printed and bound in Singapore.

The Official Rod Stewart Fan Club
UK: PO Box 241, Telford. Shropshire,
England.
North America: PO Box 66043, Unicity Postal
Outlet, Winnipeg, Manitoba, R3K 2E7.

PREFACE

& AUTHOR'S ACKNOWLEDGEMENTS

*I*n an age when the megastars of rock regularly operate in four year cycles of albums, world tours and ever increasing periods of withdrawal in between, Rod Stewart is a remarkable anomaly. After over 25 years' touring and making records he's still a grafter: rarely does a 12 month period go by without some Stewart appearances somewhere in the world and the same quarter century has seen Rod release 17 solo albums of original material and a further seven on which, as lead singer in a band, he has played a dominant creative role.

This work rate has been largely overlooked thanks to Rod's unfortunate image as a jet-setting rock playboy and incorrigible womaniser. It's a preoccupation, probably motivated by envy, that stems from the youth and/or physical comeliness of his various partners, but Rod wasn't the first rock star to have beautiful models for girl friends and he certainly won't be the last. Nevertheless, when you regularly court or marry the kind of girls that tabloid newspapers like to feature on their front pages, you can't expect to escape the banal and often embarrassing press coverage that accompanies paparazzi pictures of celebrities with their children and carry-on luggage.

Along with Joe Cocker, Rod Stewart is among the greatest interpretative singers that Britain has produced but unlike Cocker he is also a fine writer, especially of meditative romantic ballads. He has long been a stage showman *par excellence* who has performed in the world's biggest arenas before hundreds of thousands of fans across the globe.

Rod Stewart's voice is as distinctive as any in rock, a rasping, gritty howl that can ride over any kind of material. Indeed, the Stewart catalogue is among the most eclectic anywhere; a myriad of different styles ranging from introspective lullabies to all-out rock via soul, r&b, disco, blues, boogie and just about everything else bar punk.

Rod Stewart: A Visual Documentary is the first book to thoroughly chronicle this hectic career, a comprehensive run-down of each move Rod has made, from playing harmonica in Jimmy Powell's Dimensions to headlining his own concerts at Wembley Stadium. I have attempted to list every gig Rod has performed, whether as a member of a band - The Dimensions, The Hoochie Coochie Men, Steam Packet, Shotgun Express, The Jeff Beck Band and The Faces - or as a solo performer, together with every other important moment in his life. There is also a full discography containing every single and album on which Rod has appeared, together with relevant chart information for the UK and US. To list Rod's chart successes worldwide would be too great an undertaking: he has, as he would probably put it himself, a very high strike rate.

For their help in compiling this Visual Documentary, the author would like to thank Colin Parker, Chris Charlesworth, Don Stewart, Ethel Burton, Gary Millard, Matthew Bourkem, Tony Bartolo, Keith Hamer, Kevin Godridge, Micky Waller, Mike Barrett, Rod Stewart and Shanlee Johnson.

Very special thanks are due to Steve and Julie Holmes who between them kept the European branch of the Official Rod Stewart Fan Club running smoothly while the author concentrated on writing and researching this book. All memorabilia and record illustrations are from Steve Holmes' personal collection.

I am also grateful to Rod Stewart, Colin Parker, Trayc Stevenson, and Mary Cadd for the use of their photographs and to the following publications from which quotes have been taken: *Billboard, Creem, Cue, Daily Express, Daily Mail, Daily Mirror, Disc & Music Echo, Los Angeles Times, Melody Maker, Music, Music Scene, Music Week, Musicians Only, New Musical Express, News Of The World, Playgirl, Q, Record Mirror, Rolling Stone, Smiler, Sunday Mirror, The Listener, The Record, The Sun, Today, Toronto Star, Zig Zag* and *Zoo World*.

John Gray, February 1992.

INTRODUCTION

Rod Stewart was born in Highgate, North London, on January 10, 1945, and christened Roderick David Stewart by his Scottish family. His father Robert, originally from Kingsport, Edinburgh, ran away to sea as a young man and on his return relocated to London where he became a builder and married a Cockney girl named Elsie.

Robert Stewart took his young bride back to Scotland where their first four children, Mary, Peggy, Don and Bob, were born. By the time their fifth child, Roderick, arrived the family had moved back to London which meant the youngest son was the only member of the brood to have been born in England, a misfortune which Rod has tended to overlook in regard to his heritage. He's been a fanatical supporter of the Scottish football team for as long as anyone cares to remember and many are the occasions when he has rued his bad luck in being born south of Hadrian's Wall. He constantly refers to himself as a Scot, taking enormous pride in his ancestry, and has often encouraged fans to attend his concerts wearing tartan scarves and carrying Scottish flags. It is not unusual for Rod to have a Scots Pipe Band circle the arena to herald his arrival on stage.

Young Roderick's childhood was fairly conventional. In the absence of any family disasters or rebellious traits, he lived contentedly above the family newsagent's shop in the busy Archway Road which links Kentish Town and Highgate in North London. Being the youngest of five, he was inevitably spoilt by his family but he was taught to respect his elders, especially his parents, to whom he would always defer regardless of the rewards and lifestyle that his illustrious singing career has brought.

His three main early interests were football, model railways and the singing star Al Jolson who was enormously popular in the twenties and thirties. His father and two brothers were football mad and, shortly after the war, they started a local team called the Highgate Redwings. Rod was encouraged to take up the game and eventually he became skilful enough to make the Middlesex Schoolboys side and to work at Brentford FC.

The second great love in the Stewart household was Al Jolson, the massively popular American Jewish baritone who often sang in blackface and whose act was as flamboyant as

ABOVE: ROD, AGED THREE. BELOW: AL JOLSON IN THE JAZZ SINGER.

many a rock star's later in the century. The Stewart family would regularly gather around the piano and sing Jolson's many hits and as Rod became older, he started to read books about Jolson and collect his records. He admired Jolson's performing style - upon which, years later, he would base his own - and was amazed at the way Jolson could reach an audience of several thousand without a microphone. Jolson, who died in 1953, was not only Rod's strongest early role model but an influence which has stayed with him throughout his life.

Rod's schooldays were spent at the William Grimshaw Secondary Modern School in Hornsey. A popular pupil and conscientious scholar who excelled at sports, he was appointed a prefect, house captain, cricket captain and soccer captain of the school team in which Ray and Dave Davies, who went on to form The Kinks, also played.

Despite what seems to have been a fairly distinguished school career, Rod's recollections of school are blunt and unhappy. "Horrific! Primary school, which is from age five to eleven, was just bearable because it was close to my home... I'm very close to my whole family. But when I went to Secondary Modern it was about five miles away and that was unbearable. I really wasn't very good at school, and I didn't like it, although I never missed a day. My favourite subject was probably history and I was very artistic, good at sketching. I was real cocky, and that obviously comes from insecurity. I was real aggressive, taking the piss out of people all the time," he once said.

Rod decided that playing professional football was the only way in which he could earn a living, so he practised his touch skills as often as possible. Music didn't enter his head until his early teens when the first blast of fifties rock'n'roll was reaching a peak. He was taken to see a concert by Bill Haley, the plumpish kiss-curled country star who recorded 'Rock Around The Clock', and although he heard records by Eddie Cochran and Elvis Presley he didn't seem unduly impressed. Not until Rod asked his father for a railway station for his model railway set, and was given a guitar instead, did his musical interests start to develop. He learnt a few chords and joined a school skiffle group called The Kool Kats alongside four other guitar players, a tea chest bassist, washboard man and drummer. Among the songs they played were skiffle favourites like 'It Takes A Worried

ROD, AGED 12.

Man', recorded by Lonnie Donegan, and 'Freight Train' which was a number five hit for Chas McDevitt's skiffle group in 1957.

Football reigned supreme, however, and when his son left school Robert Stewart's ambitions for him centred on the soccer pitch. After a brief stint as a silk-screen printer, Rod fulfilled his father's dreams and signed apprentice papers with Brentford FC in West London. It was no picnic. Rod was expected to get up at seven in the morning and spend more time cleaning the first team's boots than kicking a football around. The vigorous training programme didn't appeal to him that much either and after only a few weeks, to the disappointment of his father, he decided to quit.

At a loss to know what to do with himself, Rod opted to see the world and headed for Paris. He hitched down to Dover and, once in France, hitched to Paris. Two days later he'd run out of money and decided the language problems were too great to overcome.

By 1962, Rod had become more and more drawn towards music. He would go and see local bands and was fast becoming interested in folk music and the left-wing politics that so often accompanied it. He grew his hair long, became a beatnik and a communist, and was a keen supporter of CND whose meetings he attended regularly. On three occasions he was arrested at sit-ins in Trafalgar Square and Whitehall and he was hauled before Bow Street magistrates and fined as a result. Rod also went on the much publicised protest marches from Aldermaston to Trafalgar Square, although he later admitted that he went for the girls rather than because of any strongly held opinions about banning the bomb! It was on these marches that Rod first sang in public, leading the crowds while strumming his guitar. At the same time he would hang out in London folk clubs and Finch's pub in Goodge Street, listening to the music of Rambling Jack Elliott, Wizz Jones and Derrol Adams. It was this music which would change his life forever.

Spurred on by his brief trip to Paris, Rod's thoughts again turned to travelling the world and his wanderlust took him to Europe once more, this time armed with a guitar. He had befriended Wizz Jones, the cult folk singer and guitarist, and with several friends in tow they decided to busk their way around the Continent. For months they made their way around Belgium, France, Italy and Spain playing American folk songs by the likes of Jack Elliott and Woody Guthrie to tourists. When they reached Barcelona, they slept beneath the arches of the football stadium and attracted the unwelcome attention of the Spanish police. Eventually Rod and his fellow beatniks were arrested and taken to the local police station. Discovering that many of the group held out-of-date passports, the British Consulate was asked to repatriate Rod and his friends. According to Rod, the Consulate sent them back to England first class on BOAC!

Returning to the family home in Highgate, Rod cut a shabby figure. His parents were unamused that their youngest son had been thrown out of Spain for vagrancy; neither were they taken with Rod's beatnik uniform which was so grubby and malodorous that Robert Stewart immediately consigned it to the fire. From henceforth Rod was obliged to find whatever work he could and in quick succession he became a grave digger, a sign-writer, a fence erector and even a newspaper delivery boy working for his father's newsagents business.

WITH FRIENDS IN 1957.

ROD IN 1963, ON THE ROAD WITH JIMMY POWELL AND THE FIVE DIMENSIONS.

"I was out of work and had to earn my keep," he recalls. "If one of the paper boys didn't turn up, my dad would kick me out of bed at 6am to do the round. It was very humiliating to be 18 and come down to find 10 year old boys working with you."

Rod's next brush with the police occurred after he became friendly with a group of beatniks who lived on a barge moored near Shoreham on the Sussex cost. They invited Rod to join them. "We were all quite happy and enjoying the sea air and not harming anyone when all of a sudden our way of life came to an end," he recalls. "Some of the local residents decided we were a blight on the neighbourhood. They complained to the police and they drove us off the barge by turning hoses on it.

"The press got the wind of this and reporters and photographers were out in force. Next day there were stories about us in the national papers. The police eventually towed the barge away and sank it to stop us going back."

The incident led to the first of Rod's press cuttings: on the front page of *The Daily Mirror*.

Rod's beatnik phase was coming to an end. Mod, which entailed dressing smartly, riding motor scooters festooned with many lights and mirrors and appreciating black soul music, was far more appealing. He became clothes conscious for the first time in his life and started to develop the enduring 'Rod The Mod' image. His love for folk developed into a love of rhythm and blues and he started to hang around Eel Pie Island near Richmond where the R&B club featured up and coming London bands like The Rolling Stones, The Yardbirds and The Birds. He now took his guitar playing more seriously and learned to play the harmonica.

In the summer of 1963 the United Kingdom was in the powerful grip of Beatlemania, the greatest pop explosion that Britain would ever experience. John, Paul, George and Ringo were everywhere, topping the charts and tapping into the nation's consciousness as no other pop group had done before them. It did not escape Rod's attention that the British music industry, led by The Beatles and their Merseybeat colleagues, was blossoming as never before. Music, he reasoned, might just pay off after all...

1963

AUTUMN

Rod joins Birmingham based band The Dimensions as backing vocalist and harmonica player. After a few weeks, blues singer Jimmy Powell hires them as his backing group and as a result Rod is no longer allowed to sing. The band, comprising Jimmy Powell (vocals), Martin Shaw (guitar), Louis Cennamo (bass), Barry Wilson (drums) and Rod (harmonica), play at

ROD
"I was just the harmonica player, and I did two numbers a night - then I went home. But to me it was great being up there on stage. I used to dress up immaculately to do my two numbers. I don't actually ever remember picking up a wage (from Powell). I think they thought, 'Oh he's a silly bastard, likes being up on stage, don't give him any money'."
(*NME*)

weddings and other social functions but their most important date is a regular Monday night booking at the Studio 51 Club in London's Newport Street owned by jazz trumpeter and bandleader Ken Colyer. The band also play dates around the UK and Jimmy Powell releases a single on Pye although Rod does not appear on the record.

At this time Rod also works for his brother Bob as a picture framer during the day.

Billed as Jimmy Powell and The Five Dimensions, Rod appears as harmonica player and plays at the following venues:

OCTOBER
Dates: Studio 51, London *(4)*, Six Bells Jazz Club, King's Road, London *(9)*, Studio 51 *(11, 14, 21 & 30)*.

NOVEMBER
Dates: Studio 51 *(11, 18 & 25)*.

DECEMBER
Dates: Studio 51 *(1, 9, 16, 23 & 30)*. Supporting The Rolling Stones on December 30.

ROD IN EARLY 1963.

JIMMY POWELL AND THE FIVE DIMENSIONS IN THE AUTUMN OF 1963. ROD IS ON THE FAR RIGHT.

1964

JANUARY

Dates: The Marquee, London *(23)*, Manor House, London *(24)*, Flamingo Club, London *(28)*, The Marquee *(30)*, Baldry's Blues Club, The Railway Hotel, Wealdstone *(31)*.

7 January

British rhythm and blues pioneer Cyril Davies, the harmonica player who led The Rhythm And Blues All Stars, dies suddenly of leukaemia.

Long John Baldry, a singer with The Rhythm And Blues All Stars, decides to keep the band going after Davies' death and looks for a new harmonica player. One night he bumps into Rod on Twickenham railway station after having played a gig at the Eel Pie Island Hotel, a regular West London blues haunt. Rod is singing drunkenly to himself as Baldry walks by.

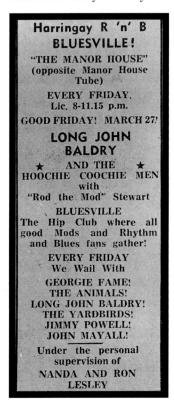

Harringay R 'n' B
BLUESVILLE!
"THE MANOR HOUSE"
(opposite Manor House Tube)
EVERY FRIDAY.
Lic. 8-11.15 p.m.
GOOD FRIDAY! MARCH 27!
LONG JOHN BALDRY
★ AND THE ★
HOOCHIE COOCHIE MEN
with
"Rod the Mod" Stewart
BLUESVILLE
The Hip Club where all good Mods and Rhythm and Blues fans gather!
EVERY FRIDAY
We Wail With
GEORGIE FAME!
THE ANIMALS!
LONG JOHN BALDRY!
THE YARDBIRDS!
JIMMY POWELL!
JOHN MAYALL!
Under the personal supervision of
NANDA AND RON LESLEY

LONG JOHN BALDRY

"I first met Rod on the London-bound platform of the Twickenham Southern Railway Station. It was a cold, damp and foggy night and the station at the time still retained vestiges of its Victorian ancestry, including gas lamp illumination. The platform was deserted, all sound quite deadened by the pea-soup fog, a perfect setting for a Gothic thriller. Suddenly, through the mist I heard the eerie sound of a harmonica being played. It was the riff from Howlin' Wolf's 'Smokestack Lightning' and it was real *natachal* blues!

"Gingerly stepping along the platform I went to investigate the source of this stirring sound, almost tripping over what I thought was a pile of old clothing spilling off a bench. When my eyes got accustomed to the gloom, I realised there was a nose protruding from the swathing of a gigantic woollen scarf.

"'Good evening,' I said to the nose. 'You strike me as being a bit of a blues fan. Your harmonica playing seems very authentic...'.

"To cut a long story short, we got chatting about music, I learned that his name was Rod and that he lived in Highgate about a mile or two from where I was living at the time, and that he had attended my show earlier that evening at the Eel Pie Hotel and had enjoyed my performance.

"I knew that I was returning to Eel Pie the following Tuesday so I invited him to come along and jam with The Hoochie Coochie Men. After the success of his short set with us, I invited him to join the band as a permanent member. Three great years of fun and larks followed!"
(Toronto Star)

They start talking about music on the train back to Waterloo and Baldry offers Rod the job of harmonica player and 'second singer' at a wage of £35 a week. This is Rod's first full-time job as a musician and he gives up his day job.

The band, comprising Rod (vocals/harmonica), Baldry (vocals), Ernie O'Malley (drums), Johnnie Parker (piano), Jeff Bradford (guitar) and Cliff Barton (bass), is called The Hoochie Coochie Men.

23 January

Long John Baldry And The Hoochie Coochie Men start a regular Thursday night residency at the Marquee. Among the songs they regularly perform are 'Night Time Is The Right Time', 'Tiger In Your Tank', 'Dimple In Your Jaw', 'I Got My Mojo Working' and 'Midnight Hour'.

25 January

Long John Baldry tells *Melody Maker*: "This is the first time I have led a group although I had a bit of experience over the past few months because Cyril was too ill to cope all the time. I know people in this band are the best blues players this side of the Atlantic, and Rod Stewart is a real find. He is one of the few teenagers who has got on to the real R&B scene."

FEBRUARY

Dates: Eyemouth, Scotland *(1)*, Dundee, Scotland *(2)*,

ABOVE: ROD'S DÉBUT SINGLE WITH LONG JOHN BALDRY AND THE HOOCHIE COOCHIE MEN.
BELOW: PERFORMING 'GOOD MORNING LITTLE SCHOOLGIRL' ON READY STEADY GO!

Baldry's Blues Club *(4)*, The Marquee, London *(6)*, Baldry's Blues Club *(10)*, The Marquee *(13)*, The Manor House *(14)*, The Gun, Croydon & Baldry's Blues Club *(18)*, The Marquee *(20)*, Leicester *(21)*, Baldry's Blues Club *(25)*, The Marquee *(27)*, The Twisted Wheel, Manchester *(29)*.

MARCH

Dates: Baldry's Blues Club *(3)*, The Marquee *(5)*, Baldry's Blues Club *(10)*, The Marquee *(13)*, Twisted Wheel *(21)*, The Marquee *(26)*, The Manor House *(27)*, Studio 51 *(28)*, Baldry's Blues Club *(31)*.

13 March

This Marquee gig is a special show supporting Sonny Boy Williamson to celebrate the re-opening of The Marquee at new premises in Wardour Street. The club was previously in Oxford Street.

APRIL

Dates: The Marquee *(2)*, Twisted Wheel *(4)*, Baldry's Blues Club *(7)*, The Marquee *(9)*, Studio 51 *(11)*, Baldry's Blues Club *(14)*, The Marquee *(16, 23 & 30 - final date of residency on April 30)*.

MAY

Dates: Studio 51 *(9)*, Northampton College, St John's Street, London *(13)*, The Marquee *(21)*, Cupiklub, Rochdale *(22)*, Stamford Hall, Altrincham *(23)*, Parr Hall, Warrington *(25)*, The Marquee *(28 - supported by Memphis Slim)*, The Rex, Wilmslow *(29)*.

30 May

Long John Baldry tells the *Melody Maker*: "I'd like to make it clear that we are a blues band and as such we dissociate ourselves from the current R&B scene. I am a blues singer with strong jazz influences, the band is a blues band and we don't play Chuck Berry or Bo Diddley stuff."

JUNE

Dates: Bromel Club, Bromley Court Hotel, Bromley *(3)*, The Marquee *(4)*, Studio 51 *(6)*, The Marquee *(11)*, The Manor House *(12)*, Studio 51 *(13)*, The Marquee *(18)*, The Marquee *(25)*, Redcar Race Course, Yorks *(26 - supporting Manfred Mann)*, The Attic Club, Hounslow *(30)*.

19 June

Rod makes his recording début duetting with Long John Baldry on Sister Rosetta Thorpe's 'Up Above My Head', the B-side of Baldry's single for United Artists 'You'll Be Mine'. The single is recorded at IBC's studio in London and produced by Jack Good. Rod receives no label credit. Long John Baldry makes an appearance on *Ready Steady Go!* to promote it.

JULY

Dates: Bromel Club *(1)*, The Marquee *(2)*, The Manor House *(3)*, Twisted Wheel *(4)*, Stamford Hall, Altrincham *(7)*, The Marquee *(9)*, The Manor House *(10)*, Twisted Wheel *(12)*, The Marquee *(16)*, The Continental, Edmonton, London *(18 - immediately after this show, The Hoochie Coochie Men move on to Studio 51 to perform at an all-nighter starting at midnight)*.

AUGUST

Dates: The Marquee *(6)*, The Manor House *(7)*, National Jazz & Blues Festival, Richmond, Surrey *(8)*, The Marquee *(13)*, Twisted Wheel *(14)*, Marquee *(20)*, Astoria,

Oldham, Lancs *(27)*, Kinky Klub, Cricklewood, London *(28)*, The Attic Club, Hounslow *(29)*, Bromel Club *(31)*.

Under the management of John Rowlands and Geoff Wright, Rod records a demonstration tape for Independent Music at a small studio in Poland Street, London. The songs, recorded in one afternoon, were 'Work Song', 'Ain't That Loving You Baby', 'Moppers Blues', 'Don't You Tell Nobody', 'Keep Your Hands Off Her', 'Just Like I Treat You' and 'Bright Lights, Big City'. Among the backing musicians are Micky Waller, Ian Armitt and Cliff Barton. All these tracks, with the exception of 'Work Song', are eventually released, without Rod's consent, during late 1976.

Decca Records staff producer Mike Vernon sees Rod perform at London's Marquee Club, and signs him to a solo deal.

6 August
Rod makes his UK TV début on *The Beat Room* with The Hoochie Coochie Men.

22 August
The Hoochie Coochie Men appear on the popular radio show *Saturday Club*, one of the few pop programmes regularly broadcast by the BBC's Light Programme.

SEPTEMBER
Dates: The Manor House *(4)*, Redcar Jazz Club *(6)*, Bromel Club *(9)*, The Marquee *(10)*, The Manor House *(11)*, Bromel Club *(16)*, The Marquee *(17)*, Stamford Hall, Altrincham *(18)*, Bromel Club, *(23 & 30)*.

10 September
Rod's first solo recording session for Decca takes place at their Number Two studio in Broadhurst Gardens, West Hampstead. Backing him are Bobby Graham (drums), Brian Daly (guitar), Reg Guest (piano) and John Paul Jones (bass).

OCTOBER
Dates: The Marquee *(1)*, Bromel Club *(7 & 14)*, The Marquee *(15)*, The Manor House *(16)*, The Marquee *(22 & 26)*.

Rod leaves The Hoochie Coochie Men following an argument with Long John Baldry. Baldry makes an unsuccessful attempt at a solo career and The Hoochie Coochie Men continue to play live with Baldry, but without Rod.

16 October
Rod débuts with the single 'Good Morning Little Schoolgirl' coupled with 'I'm

ROD WITH THE SOUL AGENTS IN DECEMBER 1964

GOOD MORNING

(LITTLE SCHOOL GIRL)

By SONNY BOY WILLIAMSON

ROD STEWART on DECCA Records

2'6 NET

Jewel Music Publishing Co. Ltd.,
50, NEW BOND STREET, LONDON, W.1
ARC MUSIC CORP., U.S.A.

23 147   Made in England

RARE SHEET MUSIC FOR ROD'S DÉBUT SINGLE
'GOOD MORNING LITTLE SCHOOLGIRL'.

PHOTO SESSION OCTOBER 1964.

PETER JONES'S NEW FACES

The feeling's there

"A WHITE person can sing the blues with just as much conviction as a Negro. All these coloured singers singing about 'Walking Down The Railroad Track' . . . they've never walked down a railroad track in their lives. Nor have I. You've got more to sing the blues about in the Archway Road, near my home, than on any railroad track I know! The speaker: **Rod Stewart,** resident of the Archway Road, London—and maker of "Good Morning Little Schoolgirl" on Decca. Talented soccer player, highly-skilled blues singer. Has worked with **Jimmy Powell** and the **Five Dimensions,** then **Long John Baldry** (as second singer)). Has played and worked with **Memphis Slim.** Has lived in a beatnik community on a derelict houseboat at Shoreham. Says, outspokenly: "Most of the third and fourth rate R and B bands are giving the music a bad name. I think most of them would be better off at home listening to **Bill Broonzy.**" Plays guitar and has busked around France and Spain with folk singer **Wiz Jones.** Was arrested there for vagrancy and sent home. A colourful six-footer, Rod's ambition is to sing with the **Count Basie Band.**

READY STEADY ROD!

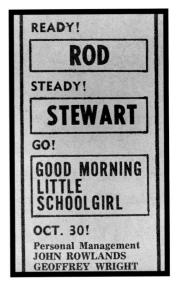

READY!
ROD
STEADY!
STEWART
GO!
GOOD MORNING LITTLE SCHOOLGIRL
OCT. 30!
Personal Management
JOHN ROWLANDS
GEOFFREY WRIGHT

Gonna Move To The Outskirts Of Town' on Decca.

To promote 'Good Morning Little Schoolgirl', Rod appears on *Ready, Steady Go!* That night he meets guitarist Ron Wood for the first time in a London pub. Wood is a member of The Birds, who are all students from West Drayton.

26 October
At tonight's Marquee gig Rod appears as a solo artist at a show billed 'An Evening With The Blues'. Also on the bill are Howlin' Wolf, Chris Barber and Long John Baldry.

DECEMBER
Dates: The Marquee, London (3, 10, 17, 24 & 31).

3 December
At this Marquee gig Rod is billed as Rod Stewart and The Ad Lib. The Ad Lib are a band managed by John Rowlands and Geoff Wright who persuade Rod to use them to back him. However, Rod doesn't feel they are right for him and declines to perform with them again.

10 December
This Marquee gig is the first London date where Rod uses the Southampton rhythm and blues band The Soul Agents, led by organist Don Shinn, to back him. Billed as Rod Stewart & The Soul Agents

they went on to appear at several clubs into early 1965.

19 December
Rod's new management announces in *Melody Maker* that Rod is resident every Thursday night at the Marquee with The Soul Agents.

24 December
Rod appears at The Marquee with The Soul Agents as support to 'Long John Baldry's Xmas Party'.

31 December
Rod is on the same Marquee bill as Sonny Boy Williamson, Long John Baldry and Chris Barber.

1965

THE CONTRACT FOR ROD'S RESIDENCY AT THE MARQUEE WITH THE SOUL AGENTS.

JANUARY
Dates: The Marquee (*7, 14, 21 & 28*).

FEBRUARY
Dates: Cooks Ferry Inn, Edmonton, London (*8*), The Marquee (*18 & 25*), The Black Prince Hotel, Bexley, Kent (*28 - supporting Buddy Guy*).

25 February
Another of the Marquee's 'An Evening With The Blues' nights where Rod is on the same bill as Buddy Guy, Long John Baldry and Chris Barber.

MARCH
Dates: Klooks Kleek, Railway Hotel, West Hampstead (*1 - supporting Buddy Guy*), The

Marquee (*26 - support to T-Bone Walker & also on the bill are Long John Baldry and Chris Barber*).

26 June
Melody Maker reports that Long John Baldry & The Hoochie Coochie Men have split up. They announce that Long John Baldry will join a new venture called The Steam Packet with Rod, Julie Driscoll and The Brian Auger Trinity.

JULY
Dates: Exeter (*16 - supporting The Rolling Stones*), Portsmouth (*17 - supporting The Rolling Stones*), Bournemouth (*18 - supporting The Rolling Stones*),

THE STEAM PACKET, LEFT TO RIGHT: LONG JOHN BALDRY, BRIAN AUGER, JULIE DRISCOLL AND ROD.

Southampton *(21)*, The Marquee *(22)*, Morecambe, Lancashire *(23)*, Two gigs in Manchester and Liverpool *(24)*, Redcar Jazz Club *(25)*, Goldhawk Club, Shepherds Bush, London *(30)*, Cleethorpes Jazz Festival *(31)*.

4 July
The Hoochie Coochie Men make their final appearance at Bexley Jazz Club.

16 July
The Steam Packet, consisting of Rod (vocals/harmonica), Julie Driscoll (vocals), Brian Auger (keyboards), Rick Brown (bass), Micky Waller (drums), Long John Baldry (vocals) and Vic Briggs (guitar) make their début supporting The Rolling Stones at a concert in Exeter. The group is the brainchild of Yardbirds' manager Giorgio Gomelski and at his suggestion, Rod and Baldry team up again to form a multi-vocal band

based on soul and rhythm'n'blues music.

Songs featured in Steam Packet's live show include 'Another Saturday Night', 'Mr Pitiful', 'The Midnight Hour', 'Dancing In The Street' and 'On Broadway'.

AUGUST
Dates: The London Palladium *(1)*, Edmonton *(2)*, Norwich *(3)*, Margate, Kent *(5)*, Guilford *(6)*, Clacton-on-Sea *(7)*, 5th National Jazz & Blues Festival, Richmond Athletic Ground, Surrey *(8)*, Klooks Kleek, Railway Hotel, West Hampstead *(10)*, Derby *(13)*, Manchester *(14)*, Ilkley, Yorks *(15)*, Chester *(16)*, Altrincham, Cheshire *(17)*, Bromel Club *(18)*, The Marquee *(19)*, Erdington, West Midlands *(20)*, Nottingham *(21)*, Twickenham, Middlesex *(22)*, Ipswich, Suffolk *(23)*, Cheltenham, Glos *(25)*, Portsmouth *(26)*, Leicester *(27)*, Bolton & Accrington,

ROD
What we were doing with Steam Packet was like a white soul revue. Like a white Ike And Tina Turner show but nowhere near as good. We never made any records because we were all on different labels. The idea of Brian Auger was to use everybody in that group to get himself off the ground." (*NME*)

Lancs *(28)*, Mr Smith's, Hanley, Stoke-on-Trent *(29)*, Redcar *(30)*.

1 August
Two London Palladium shows the same day supporting The Rolling Stones; also on the bill are The Walker Brothers, The Moody Blues, The Quiet Five, The Fourmost and Julie Grant.

6 August
The Steam Packet appear on *Ready Steady Go!* and in the evening play a concert at Guildford, Surrey.

SEPTEMBER

Dates: The Marquee *(2)*, Greenford, London *(3)*, Watford, Herts *(4)*, Stockport, Cheshire *(5)*, Edmonton *(6)*, Norwich *(8)*, Rochdale, Lancs *(9)*, Derby *(10)*, Rawdon, Yorks *(11)*, Coventry, Warwicks *(12)*, Southsea, Hants *(13)*, Bristol *(14)*, Carpenders Park, Watford *(15)*, Oldham, Lancs *(16)*, Troutbeck, Ilkley, Yorks *(17)*, Lowestoft *(18)*, The Black Prince Hotel, Bexley *(19)*, Solihull, Warwicks *(20)*, Swindon, Wilts *(24)*, Nottingham *(25)*, Kirklevington, Yorks *(26)*, Sheffield, Yorks *(27)*, Marquee *(30)*.

OCTOBER

Dates: Twickenham *(1)*, East Grinstead, Sussex *(2)*, Hayes, Middlesex *(3)*, Klooks Kleek *(5)*, Sheffield *(6)*, Cleethorpes, Lincs *(7)*, Birmingham *(8)*, Manchester *(9)*, Sheffield *(10)*, Klooks Kleek *(12)*, The Marquee *(14)*, The Cellar Club, Kingston, Surrey *(15)*, Portsmouth *(16)*, Hayes *(17)*, Warrington *(18)*, Cheltenham, Glos *(20)*, Scotch Club, London *(21)*, Scotch Club & The Manor House, London *(22)*, Prestatyn, N. Wales *(23)*, Hanley, Stoke-on-Trent *(24)*, Norwich *(26)*, Bromel Club *(27)*, The Marquee *(28)*, Newcastle *(29)*, Liverpool *(30)*, Carlisle, Cumberland *(31)*.

NOVEMBER

Dates: Reading, Berks *(1)*, Bristol *(2)*, Stockport, Cheshire *(5)*, Banbury, Oxon *(6)*, Black Prince Hotel, Bexley, *(7)*, St. Martin's Baths Hall, Ipswich, Suffolk *(8)*, Floral Hall, Gorleston, Norfolk *(9)*, BRC Social Club, Stafford *(11)*, University, York *(12)*, Club A Gogo, Newcastle *(13)*, Coatham Hotel, Redcar *(14)*, Town Hall, Farnborough, Hants, *(17)*, Il Rondo, Leicester *(19)*, Twisted Wheel *(20)*, Leofric Hotel, Coventry *(21)*, Cooks Ferry Inn, Edmonton *(22)*, The Marquee *(23)*, Beachcomber, Bolton *(24)*, Beachcomber, Preston *(25)*, University, Lancaster *(26)*, Dancing Slipper, Nottingham *(27)*, Blue Moon, Hayes *(28)*, Klooks Kleek *(30)*.

2 November

Rod stars in his own television special titled *An Easter With Rod*, a 30-minute portrait of a typical mod. It is screened by Rediffusion.

15 November

Tyne Tees TV *Steam Packet Show.*

19 November

Columbia release Rod's second solo single entitled 'The Day Will Come' backed with 'Why Does It Go On?'

DECEMBER

Dates: Bromel Club *(1)*, Swansea, S. Wales *(2 & 3)*, Cheltenham, *(4)*, Corn Exchange, Bristol *(7)*, Goldsmiths' College, Lewisham, London *(9)*, Manor House *(10)*, Starlite Club, Wembley *(11)*, Mr Smith's, Hanley *(12)*, Art College, Crayford, Kent *(13)*, King's College, London *(14)*, Coatham Hotel, Redcar *(16)*, The Dungeon, Nottinghan & Town Hall, Birmingham *(17)*, St Georges Hotel, Hinckley, Leics *(18)*, Twisted Wheel, Manchester *(19)*, The Marquee *(13)*, Birmingham *(24)*, St. Martin's Baths Hall, Ipswich *(27)*, Mojo, Sheffield *(31)*.

THE STEAM PACKET ON STAGE.

1966

JANUARY
Dates: Middlesborough, Yorks *(1)*, Kirklevington *(2)*, Billingham *(4)*, Coventry *(5)*, Manchester *(7)*, Ramsgate, Kent *(8)*, Klooks Kleek *(11)*, Bromel Club *(12)*, The Marquee *(13)*, Nottingham *(14)*, Chelsea, London *(15)*, Reading *(17)*, Bristol *(18)*, Leicester *(21)*, Manchester *(22)*, Coventry *(23)*, Wood Green, London *(25)*, Southampton *(26)*, The Marquee *(27)*, Northampton *(28)*, University, Nottingham *(29)*, Hayes *(30)*.

FEBRUARY
Dates: Norwich *(2)*, Newcastle *(3)*, Birmingham *(4)*, Leeds *(5)*, Birmingham *(6)*, Watford, Herts *(7)*, The Marquee *(10)*, Exeter *(11)*, Camberley, Surrey *(7&12)*, Hanley *(13)*, Liverpool *(14)*, Klooks Kleek *(15)*, Cromwellian Club *(16)*, Cleethorpes *(17)*, University, Warwick *(19)*, Ipswich *(21)*, Grays *(22)*, The Marquee *(24)*, Uxbridge *(26)*, Woolwich *(27)*, Edmonton *(28)*.

MARCH
Date: Klooks Kleek *(17)*.

12 March
Melody Maker reports that Rod has left The Steam Packet to go solo.

17 March
At this Klooks Keel one-off show Rod appears with The Peter B's, aka Peter B's Looners, who comprise Peter Bardens on keyboards, Peter Green on guitar, Dave Ambrose on bass and Mick Fleetwood on drums. They are billed as 'The Peter B's with guest singer Rod Stewart'.

15 April
Columbia release Rod's third single, a cover of the Sam Cooke song 'Shake' backed with 'I Just Got Some'.

MAY
Dates: Jigsaw Club, Manchester *(28)*, Flamingo Club, London *(29)*.

Rod joins The Shotgun Express. Line-up is Rod (vocals), Beryl Marsden (vocals), Dave Ambrose (bass), Peter Green (guitar), Mick Fleetwood (drums) and Peter Bardens (keyboards). Peter Green, who soon joins John Mayall's Bluesbreakers, is replaced by Jon Morshead who in turn is replaced by Phil Sawyer.

Peter Bardens: "Peter B's Looners just weren't diverse or remunerative enough to remain a viable proposition - so we restructured the group with Rod Stewart and Beryl Marsden and became Shotgun Express which was reasonably successful for a few months. After a while it lost momentum: Phil often didn't appear for gigs, Beryl was always at the hairdressers, Rod was always in bed, and the administration got to be

too great a problem. It didn't matter where we were playing - we never left for a gig before four o'clock - so we were always late. Good group, though."

Among the songs played by Shotgun Express are 'Hold On I'm Coming', 'Knock On Wood', 'Midnight Hour', Feel So Good', '6345789 - That's My Number', 'Soulful Dress' and 'High Heel Sneakers'.

THE SHOTGUN EXPRESS, LEFT TO RIGHT: ROD, BERYL MARSDEN AND PETER BARDENS.

JUNE

Dates: Flamingo Club *(4)*, The Ram Jam Club, Brixton, London *(18)*, Black Prince Hotel *(19)*, Marquee *(20)*, The Manor House *(24)*, Bromel Club *(26)*.

JULY

The Steam Packet play their final dates, without Rod, in St Tropez.

AUGUST

Dates: Jigsaw Club, Manchester *(6)*, Klooks Kleek *(16)*, Flamingo Club, London *(19* - two sets at 7.30pm and midnight)*, The Ram Jam Club, Brixton, London (7.30pm) & Flamingo Club, London (midnight) *(20)*, Black Prince Hotel, Bexley *(21)*, Flamingo Club, London *(27* - two sets at 7.30pm and midnight)*.

Rod records the Goffin/King song 'Come Home Baby' with P. P. Arnold. Produced by Mick Jagger, it wasn't released until 1975 when it appeared on the Springboard label's 'Rod Stewart & The Faces' album.

SEPTEMBER

Dates: Corn Exchange, Bedford *(6)*, Public Hall, Harpenden, Herts *(8)*, Manor House *(9)*, Stoke Hotel, Guildford *(15)*,

OCTOBER

Dates: Twisted Wheel *(8)*, Ram Jam Club *(29)*.

21 October

The Shotgun Express début on Columbia with the single 'I Could Feel The Whole World Turn Round Underneath Me' backed with the instrumental 'Curtains'.

NOVEMBER

Dates: Technical College, Hull *(11)*, Technical College, Sunderland *(12)*, St. Georges, Hinckley, Leics *(13)*, Tigers Head, Catford *(18)*, Rikky Tick, Hounslow *(19)*, The Ram Jam Club (7.30) & Flamingo Club (midnight) *(26)*, Bridge Boat, Nottingham *(27)*, The Star, Croydon *(28)*, Barratt's Youth Centre, South Ockendon *(29)*.

DECEMBER

Date: Klooks Kleek *(27)*.

ROD CIRCA 1966

1967

JANUARY
Date: The Ram Jam Club *(13)*.

28 January
Record Mirror reports that Rod has been rehearsing with ace guitarist Jeff Beck who recently left The Yardbirds, Viv Prince (of The Pretty Things) and Jet Harris (formerly with The Shadows).

FEBRUARY
The Jeff Beck Group is formed with Rod on vocals, Beck on guitar, Ron Wood on bass and Roger Cook on drums after Viv Prince and Jet Harris proved unsuitable. Roger Cook does not stay long enough to play any gigs and is soon replaced by Rod Coombes. Throughout their two and half year life, The Jeff Beck Group would go through six drummers: Viv Prince, Roger Cook, Rod Coombes, Aynsley Dunbar, Micky Waller and finally Tony Newman.

Rod Coombes later played with Juicy Lucy and Stealer's Wheel.

According to Rod, his involvement with Beck came out of sympathy for him. "We thought we'd better help him out... I mean, for a guitar player like that to come out with a thing like 'Hi Ho Silver Lining' - it was a crime."

The formation of the group didn't halt the deliberately commercialised singles. Beck's follow up to 'Hi Ho' was a Graham Gouldman song called 'Tallyman'. The B-side 'Rock My Plimsoul' was more indicative of The Jeff Beck Group's true worth.

3 March
The newly-formed Jeff Beck Group make a disastrous début at the Finsbury Park Astoria on the opening night of a package tour with The Small Faces and Roy Orbison. *Melody Maker* reports: "The group were obviously under rehearsed and in the first house on the opening night Jeff walked off stage when the power failed. Rod Stewart attempted to salvage what remained of the act. In the second house they played badly and created a very poor impression."

Drummer Rod Coombes is immediately sacked and replaced by Aynsley Dunbar. The band drop out of the tour and spend some time knocking themselves into better shape.

MAY
Dates: Meacham Public Hall (*7* - opening date of Jeff Beck

Group's first tour of ballrooms and clubs), Britannia, Nottingham *(10)*, Town Hall, High Wycombe *(12)*, Feathers, Ealing *(15)*, Corn Exchange, Bristol *(16)*, Victoria Hall, Selkirk *(19)*, Market Hall, Carlisle *(20)*, University, Liverpool *(25)*, Shoreline, Bognor *(27)*, Tabernacle, Stockport *(28)*, Oxford Cellar, Norwich *(31)*.

JULY
Date: Saville Theatre, London (*2* - on the same bill as Cream and John Mayall's Bluesbreakers).

7 July
Jeff Beck releases the instrumental 'Tallyman' backed with 'Rock My Plimsoul' which features Rod on vocal. It charts at No 30 in the UK.

AUGUST
Dates: 7th National Jazz & Blues Festival at The Royal Windsor

THE JEFF BECK GROUP, LEFT TO RIGHT: ROD, JEFF BECK, RON WOOD AND AYNSLEY DUNBAR.

THE JEFF BECK GROUP.

1968

JANUARY
Date: Norwich *(27)*.

FEBRUARY
Dates: Egham, Surrey *(3)*, Nottingham *(9)*, Hammersmith, London *(17)*.

5 February
Recording session.

10 February
Jeff Beck releases the instrumental 'Love Is Blue' backed with 'I've Been Drinking Again' which features Rod on vocal. It charts at No 23 in the UK.

MARCH
Dates: Manchester *(2)*, Rotterdam, Holland *(3)*, Dartford, Kent *(8)*, Mill Hill & Covent Garden, London *(9)*, Oswestry *(15)*, Chesham, Bucks *(16)*, Grantham *(17)*, Walthamstow, London *(22)*, Bletchley *(23)*, Nottingham *(24)*, Wolverhampton *(30)*.

Newly signed to Immediate Records, Rod releases a solo single titled 'Little Missunderstood' backed with 'So Much To Say'. It is not a hit.

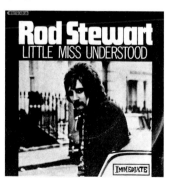

20 March
Recording session.

APRIL
Dates: Cleethorpes *(1)*,

Racecourse *(13)*, Dunstable *(19)*, Guildford, Surrey *(20)*, Worthing, East Sussex *(24)*, Folkestone, Kent *(26)*, Woburn Abbey Festival *(28)*.

SEPTEMBER
Dates: Manchester *(2)*, Stockport, Cheshire *(3)*, Malvern *(5)*, Rugby *(8)*, Lowestoft *(9)*, Nottingham *(15)*, Bracknell, Berkshire *(16)*, Chertsey, Surrey *(17)*, Hartlepool *(22)*, Edmonton, London *(25)*, The Marquee *(26)*, Dartford, Kent, & Chalk Farm, London *(29)*, Hinckley, Leics *(30)*.

OCTOBER
Dates: Swansea *(6)*, Leeds *(7)*, Ghent, Belgium *(13)*, Reading *(14)*, Guildford *(15)*, Southampton *(21)*, The Speakeasy, London *(26)*, Tamworth *(27)*, Kirklevington *(29)*, Coventry *(30)*.

9 October
The Jeff Beck Group make a broadcast on BBC Radio 1.

NOVEMBER
Dates: Poole, Dorset *(3)*, Exeter, Devon *(4)*, Nottingham *(10)*, Matlock, Derby *(11)*, Newcastle *(16)*, Coventry *(18)*, Haverfordwest *(25)*, Salisbury *(30)*.

DECEMBER
Dates: Cardiff *(1)*, Romsey, Hants *(2)*, Birmingham *(8)*, Kingston, Surrey *(9)*, Slough *(11)*, The Marquee *(12)*, University, Sussex *(14)*, Walthamstow, London *(15)*, Dereham, Norfolk *(16)*, Oxford *(23)*.

5 & 7 December
The Jeff Beck Group enter the studio to record a new single. By this time Micky Waller has taken over on drums.

JEFF BECK
"Rod Stewart, our lead singer was in despair. I was the only one who had been to the States before and the boys were all scared stiff. Rod hid behind the amplifiers when he was singing. The audience were amazed, they thought I was a ventriloquist."

ROD
"I suffered from the most frightening experience... the voice just went. It was just stage fright I suppose. I just went to open my mouth on 'Ain't Superstitious' and nothing came out. So I remember in those days Woody and I used to have a little bag we carried around with us all the time and it used to have a little bottle of brandy in it. So I ran back, got the bag, had a quick shot of brandy and then picked up the mike and it all came out. But it was just stage fright. I sort of crouched behind the amp and had a quick swig. Beck was covering for me, he was playing a solo, but there was definitely a sort of embarrassment all round... everyone was looking for the singer. And sure enough, as the brandy hit the blood stream, back came the vocals."

Llanelly, Wales *(4)*, Bicester *(5)*, Bexley *(7)*, Bath *(8)*, The Marquee *(9)*, Worthing *(11)*, Chur, Switzerland *(15)*, Lucerne, Switzerland *(16)*, St Gallen, Switzerland *(17)*, Copenhagen, Denmark & Trelleborg, Sweden *(20)*, Copenhagen & Roskilde, Denmark *(21)*, Gothenburg, Sweden *(24)*, Uddevalla & Stockholm, Sweden *(25)*,

Jönköping, Sweden *(26)*, Kristinehamn, Sweden *(27)*, Copenhagen *(28)*.

15 April
The Jeff Beck Group tour Switzerland, Sweden, Denmark and France, opening in Chur. They also appear on a TV show in Zurich.

MAY
Dates: Paris, France *(4 & 5)*, Dartford, Kent *(10)*, Bradford *(11)*, Kirklevington *(12)*, Weston-super-Mare *(18)*.

14, 15, 16 & 25 May
Recording sessions.

JUNE
Dates: Coventry *(2)*, Manor House *(7)*, Fillmore East, New York, NY *(14, 15, 18, 19, 20, 21 & 22)*, Boston, Mass *(26, 27, 28, & 29)*.

14 June
The Jeff Beck Group begin an eight week tour of America at the Fillmore East, New York.

They are accompanied for much of the tour by Beck's former colleague in The Yardbirds, guitarist Jimmy Page, who will shortly form Led Zeppelin, and his manager Peter Grant, both of whom note with interest the reaction that Beck's group and style of music inspire in the US.

28 June
New Musical Express reports that Jeff Beck and Rod Stewart have been receiving standing ovations at concerts during their US tour and... 'have pulled record business equalling that of Jimi Hendrix and The Doors.'

JULY
Dates: Dearborn University, Detroit, Mi *(5 & 6)*, Ann Arbor, Mi *(7)*, Cleveland,

ROD
"In the early days, I always felt overshadowed by Beck's guitar playing, but towards the end of the band, when we were beginning to be successful, the guitar and vocal bit used to fit like a glove, we really used to have it off tight. And if Jeff was having a bad night then I'd leap around a bit more and if I'd lost my voice then he'd do the same thing for me. We had a great rapport between the two of us."

Ohio *(9, 10 & 11)*, Houston, Tx *(12 & 13)*, Dallas, Tx *(17)*, Fillmore West, San Francisco, Ca *(19, 20, 21, 23, 24 & 25)*, Shrine Auditorium, Los Angeles, Ca *(26 & 27)*.

AUGUST
Dates: Shrine Auditorium, Los Angeles, Ca *(2 & 3)*, Kempton Park Racecourse, Sunbury *(10 - on the same bill as The Nice, Ten Years After and Arthur Brown)*.

24 August
The début Jeff Beck album 'Truth' enters the US charts at No 163.

SEPTEMBER
Dates: The Manor House, London *(6)*, Norwich *(14)*, Stockholm, Sweden *(30)*.

17 September
The Jeff Beck Group record a session for the BBC Radio One *Top Gear* programme.

18 September
Recording session.

30 September
The Jeff Beck Group start a series of dates in Sweden and Denmark with a concert in Stockholm.

THE BECK GROUP LIVE ON STAGE AT NEW YORK'S FILLMORE EAST, JUNE 1968.

OCTOBER
Dates: Stockholm *(1, 2 & 3)*, Jönköping, Sweden *(4)*, Copenhagen, Denmark *(5)*, Chicago, Ill *(11)*, Alma, Mi *(12)*, Cleveland, Ohio *(13)*, Fillmore East, New York, NY *(18 & 19)*, Alexandra, NY *(20)*, Boston, Mass *(22, 23 & 24)*, Philadelphia, Pa *(25 & 26)*, Toronto, Ontario *(27)*.

4 October
The Jeff Beck Group release their first album 'Truth' which reaches No 15 in the US but fails to chart in the UK.

8 October
Rod Stewart signs a solo recording contract with the London-based American producer Lou Reizner.

ROD
"It was a great band to sing with but I couldn't take all the aggravation and unfriendliness that developed. It was getting too ridiculous for words near the end - we were trying to hide from each other all the time. One would stay at the Hilton and the others would stay at Hotel Third-on-the-bill around the corner. In the two and a half years I was with Beck I never once looked him in the eye... I always looked at his shirt or something like that."
(Zig Zag)

LOU REIZNER
"I saw Rod perform with Jeff, and then we happened to be staying at the same hotel and we got to be mates. His appearance was so different... he always used to wear clothes that he had out-grown. Like he would be popping out the buttons of his shirt and he always had that same hair-do, and used to wear trousers that came down to just above his ankles - it was totally his own style of dress. There was no-one else who looked like that."
(The Rod Stewart Story, George Tremlett)

11 October
The Jeff Beck Group start their second US tour in Chicago.
The set for this tour includes the following: 'Plynth', 'Bye Bye (Baby Goodbye)', 'I've Got The Sweetest Little Angel', 'Stoned Crazy', 'Ain't Superstitious', '(I Know) I'm Losing You', 'Rock My Plimsoul', 'Let Me Love You', 'Shapes Of Things', 'Loving You Is Sweeter Than Ever', 'You Shook Me', 'Jailhouse Rock', 'Rice Pudding' and 'Beck's Bolero'.

NOVEMBER
Dates: Detroit, Mi *(1, 2 & 3)*, Houston, Tx *(8)*, Dallas, Tx *(9)*, Oklahoma City, Ok *(10)*, Miami, Fla *(15 & 16)*, Cleveland, Ohio *(22 & 23)*, Seattle, Wash *(27)*, Los Angeles, Ca *(29 & 30)*.

DECEMBER
Dates: Fillmore West, San Francisco, Ca *(5, 6, 7 & 8)*, Middle Earth Club, The Roundhouse, London *(21)*.

1969

JANUARY
Date: Marquee *(14)*.

Nicky Hopkins joins The Jeff Beck Group on keyboards.

FEBRUARY
Date: The Tallyho, Tolworth, Surrey *(5)*.

Jeff Beck fires Ron Wood and Micky Waller, claiming that their playing has deteriorated. This occurs during the recording of 'Beck Ola' and comes as a shock to Rod who believes that Beck was behind Wood's removal and Hopkins behind Waller's removal.

ROD
"By that time Ronnie was well pissed off and from then on he just used the group as filler while he looked for another band."
(Zig Zag)

MARCH
The new line-up of The Jeff Beck Group fly to America to pick up on a tour that was partially cancelled due to the changes in the band. The group now includes Beck, Rod and Nicky Hopkins from the old band and newcomers drummer Tony Newman (formerly with Sounds Incorporated) and bassist Douglas Blake. After one gig in Virginia, Blake is sacked and Ron Wood re-hired and flown over.

JEFF BECK IN 1968.

APRIL
Date: The Lyceum, London *(25)*.

3 May
New Musical Express reports that Steve Marriott has left The Small Faces and a replacement is being sought.

JUNE
Date: Marquee *(6)*.

Rod makes his first public appearance with The Faces at a Cambridge University ball. They appear billed as Quiet Melon and are led by Ron Wood's elder brother, Art.

A second gig as Quiet Melon takes place at a college in Surrey with a line-up that includes Art Wood, Long John Baldry and Jimmy Horowitz.

IAN McLAGAN
"It was one of those end of term balls - all champagne and strawberries and jugs of beer and roast beef dinners. The food was free and we were given a hundred quid to split between us. It was a joke. We went on without any rehearsal, with hardly any equipment. Rod came on and sang a couple of numbers. It was a general piss-up."

7 June
The Small Faces announce that the replacement for Steve Marriott is Ron Wood.

Melody Maker reports that

Rod has signed a solo deal with Mercury Records but will still be a part of The Jeff Beck Group.

JULY
Rod leaves The Jeff Beck Group after an unhappy two and a half years.

10 July
Rod goes into the recording studio with Lou Reizner to record his first solo album for Mercury records.

5 September
The Jeff Beck Group, although now dissolved, release a new

SMALL FACES IN 1969, IAN McLAGAN, RONNIE LANE, KENNY JONES AND STEVE MARRIOT.

album titled 'Beck Ola'. It reaches No 39 in the UK charts and No 15 in the US charts.

18 October
Rod Stewart is announced as The Small Faces' new singer. The group's full complement is Rod on vocals, Ron Wood on guitar, Ronnie Lane on bass, Ian McLagan on keyboards and Kenny Jones on drums.

NOVEMBER
The Small Faces play dates in Switzerland.

1 November
New Musical Express reports that Rod has been given special dispensation by Mercury Records to record with The Small Faces on Warner Brothers.

20 December
The newly re-formed Small Faces announce their first UK dates at Sheffield, Norwich and Bristol.

IAN McLAGAN
"We were a little worried about asking Rod to join because we didn't want to get into the situation where he would be the front man and we would just end up playing behind him. We had gone through all that with Steve Marriott in The Small Faces. I'm not knocking Steve, because I think he's a great performer, but I think we just all let him take all the credit for everything. Eventually Kenny asked Rod to join but not before we had tried to do the vocals ourselves. We were quite pathetic at singing so it was a case of having to get a singer."

1970

JANUARY

Dates: University, Sheffield *(17)*, Mothers, Birmingham *(25)*.

Rod makes a promotional tour of the US billed as 'Rod Stewart Visits His Friends'. The tour concentrates on

ROD
"This Mercury tour has gone very smoothly. Some of it can be a real drag, like the interviews where each person asks the same questions. I try to think of different ways of phrasing the answers so I don't repeat myself, but sometimes you just run out of ideas. I'm very pleased that Mercury allowed me to record with The Small Faces and the promotion tour will help promote The Small Faces and myself. Plus it should help increase sales of my current Mercury album.

"Some of the biggest problems on a promotional tour can come from the record company sponsoring it. When I was with Beck, some of the people at Epic Records really messed up the group. Some thought I was Jeff or Jeff was me. It was really embarrassing sometimes to have to explain that I didn't play guitar with the group. Another thing was that in some cities the promotion men would set up interviews with people who didn't have the slightest idea who we were. Newspaper people and 'Top 40' DJs didn't know us and couldn't care less."
(Billboard)

visiting FM progressive rock stations, underground papers and pop music editors of the regular press. The tour takes him to most major markets coast to coast.

Later in the month the newly constituted Small Faces embark on an endless tour around Britain to establish their own identity. At first it's a surprisingly uphill struggle but their laisser-faire attitude of boozy good times for all eventually wins them a huge following.

FEBRUARY

Dates: Top Rank Suite, Southampton *(2)*, The Lyceum, London *(6)*, University, Norwich *(13)*, University, Bristol *(27)*.

Shortening their name to The Faces, the group release their début single 'Flying' backed with 'Three Button Hand Me Down'. Despite good reviews and an appearance on *Top Of The Pops*, it fails to chart.

13 February
Rod's first album 'An Old Raincoat Won't Ever Let You Down' is released. He started

RONNIE LANE
"We came out of The Small Faces in debt but now we're square and earning money. We didn't really want to put a single out, but our new record company said if we were good boys, there'd be some money in the bin for us. 'Flying' is more a trailer for the album than anything else - we don't really care if it is a hit but it would be nice if it was." *(RM)*

recording the LP while he was still a member of The Jeff Beck Group and before he made his last US tour with them. It fails to chart in the UK but makes No 139 in the US where, thanks to the success of The Jeff Beck Group, Rod has a higher profile than at home.

27 February
Kenny Jones tells *Melody Maker*: "The new group has done about six gigs so far and they were really good. The band is nothing like the old Faces. Only the name is the same. The music is completely different. Some of us wanted to change the name of the group completely so we all

ROD
"I was offered the chance to make 'An Old Raincoat Won't Ever Let You Down' while I was with Jeff (Beck), but I first turned it down because I didn't want to offend him. That album was really jumping in at the deep end - I produced it as well. The only success I've ever had was doing things off my own bat and not listening to producers and record companies. I wrote a lot of the numbers. I thought 'something desperate's got to be done,' so I told people what sort of sound I wanted then I'd bring home the tape without the vocals on it and write words to fit the sounds. It was a strange way of going about things, but it worked." *(Disc & Music Echo)*

THE FACES IN EARLY 1970, LEFT TO RIGHT: RONNIE LANE, KENNY JONES, ROD STEWART, RON WOOD AND IAN McLAGAN.

agreed to keep it as The Faces, without the Small bit.

"At the gigs the kids haven't really been expecting old material. They don't really know what to expect. We've got to get together a bit more, but the gigs have been really exciting.

"We've been rehearsing five or six hours a night in a warehouse in South London. In a way I'm glad the old group split because it gave us all a chance to do something new."

MARCH

Dates: Lyceum *(1)*, Mothers, Birmingham *(21)*, Varsity Arena, Toronto, Canada *(25)*.

The Faces release their début album 'First Step'. It charts at No 45 in the UK and No 119 in the US.

1 March

This Lyceum date is billed as The Faces' first London performance, although they had played the same venue the month before as The Small Faces. Included in the set are

faces.

SUNDAY LYCEUM
STRAND, W.C.2

First London Performance

FACES

'Wicked Messenger', 'Devotion', 'The Evil', 'Stone', 'Pineapple & The Monkey', 'Flying', 'Plynth' and 'Three Button Hand Me Down'. 'Stone' features Rod on banjo.

14 March

The Faces guest on BBC2's *Disco 2*.

25 March

The Faces make their North American début at the Varsity Arena, Toronto, Canada. They are third on the bill to Canned Heat and The MC5. The date is part of a 28-concert tour of America which lasts until late May.

The Faces find themselves in the unusual position of being

SMALL FACES

GREASE BAND

SAVOY BROWN

more popular in America than in Britain, partly because American fans revere Rod as the former singer with The Jeff Beck Group, partly because

The Faces' music and attitude is more attuned to American tastes and partly because of the rabid Anglophobia that influenced the tastes of American rock fans in the late Sixties and early Seventies.

APRIL

Dates: East Town Theater, Detroit Mi *(3 & 4)*, Ungano's, New York *(8 & 9)*, Electric Factory, Philadelphia Pa *(10 & 11)*, Beaver's, Chicago, Ill *(15 & 16)*, Palladium, Birmingham, Mi *(17 & 18)*, Boston Garden, Boston Mass *(20)*, Warehouse, Ithaca, NY *(23)*, Action House, Island Park, NY *(24 & 25)*.

MAY

Dates: Eastown, Detroit Mi *(1 & 2)*, Fillmore West, San Francisco, Ca *(7, 8, 9 & 10)*, Eagles Ballroom, Seattle, Wash *(15 & 16)*, Garden Auditorium, Vancouver, BC *(17)*, Olympic Theater, Los Angeles, Ca *(22)*, Fillmore East, New York, NY *(29 & 30)*.

JUNE

Dates: Civic Centre, Dunstable *(20)*, Mothers, Birmingham *(27)*.

AUGUST

Dates: Atlantic City, NJ *(7, 8, 9 & 10)*, Lyceum *(21)*.

August 7 - 10

The Faces' four concerts in USA's Atlantic City earn a reported $30,000. They then fly direct to Scandinavia for three days of concerts.

SEPTEMBER

Dates: The Country Club, Hampstead, London *(11)*, Black Prince Hotel *(13)*, Lyceum *(18)*, Marquee *(25)*.

The Faces are featured in the

film *London Rock* which is networked throughout America by Metromedia TV. In *Melody Maker* Roy Hollingworth writes: "The best thing I've ever seen Rod do was for a little documentary called *London Rock*. There's this American commentary trying to do the big star bit with The Faces: 'Here's Rod Stewart arriving in his Lamborghini'. And Rod pulls up, gets out and pulls a face, then does the whole smooth job. Later in the film he sits in a field with a dog and guitar and sings 'Nobody Knows' - just voice, guitar and barking dog. That's Rod Stewart and he's brilliant."

'It's All Over Now' backed with 'Jo's Lament' is released as Rod's new single by Vertigo. Both tracks are featured on the forthcoming album 'Gasoline Alley', although 'It's All Over Now' is a different mix from the album version.

11 September
Rod releases his second solo album entitled 'Gasoline Alley'. It charts at No 62 in the UK and No 27 in the US, again reflecting the disparity in popularity that Rod enjoys on each side of the Atlantic.

OCTOBER
Dates: Plainfield, Vt *(1)*, Capitol Theater, Porchester, NY *(2 & 3)*, Boston Tea Party, Boston, Mass *(5 & 7)*, The Club, Rochester, NY *(9)*, Wagner College, Staten

ROD
"Gasoline Alley is somewhere in San Francisco. I got the idea from a girl at the Fillmore. We were talking and she said something like, "I must get home, because my mother will say, 'Where have you been, down Gasoline Alley?' And I said, 'What?' Gasoline Alley is nowhere in particular to me. It was about a feeling I had when I was in Spain, and I couldn't get back to England. I wanted to get back to England, but I didn't have the money to get back. So it's a song about going home; I've experienced that. 'Jo's Lament' is a song about a girl I put in a family way, and 'Lady Day' is very true, about a girl I fell in love with a long time ago and she didn't want to know me."
(*Rolling Stone*)

Island, NY *(10)*, Kingston Armory, Wilkes Barre, Pa *(12)*, East Town Theater, Detroit, Mi *(16 & 17)*, The Scene, Milwaukee, Wis *(18)*, Spectrum, Philadelphia, Pa *(23)*, Action House, Island Park, NY *(24)*, Palladium, Birmingham, Mi *(27)*, Fillmore West, San Francisco, Ca *(28)*, Santa Monica Civic Auditorium, Ca *(30)*, Agridome, Vancouver, BC *(31)*.

October 1
The Faces start their second US tour at Goddard College, Plainfield, Vermont. The set for this tour varies from night to night and is made up from: 'Devotion', 'I Don't Wanna Discuss It', 'Flying', 'Wicked Messenger', 'Country Comfort', 'I Wanna Be Loved', 'Cut Across Shorty', 'Plynth', 'Honky Tonk Woman', 'Gasoline Alley', 'It's All Over Now', 'Love In Vain', 'I Feel So Good', 'Had Me A Real Good Time', 'Blues Deluxe', 'Shake, Shudder, Shiver', 'The Evil', 'Nobody Knows', 'Pineapple & The Monkey', 'Maybe I'm Amazed'.

N O V E M B E R
Dates: Dewey's, Madison, Wis *(3)*, State University Of New York, Stoney Brook, NY *(5)*, Williams College, Williamstown, Mass *(6)*, Olympia Stadium, Detroit, Mi *(7)*, The Depot, Minneapolis, Minn *(8)*, Fillmore East, New York City, NY *(10)*, The Club, Rochester, NY *(11)*, Syndrome, Chicago, Ill *(13)*, Hara Arena, Dayton, Ohio *(14)*, Commodore Ballroom, Lowell, Mass *(15)*, Marquee *(20)*, Wake Arms, Epping, Essex *(22)*, University, Leicester *(28)*, The Greyhound, Croydon, Surrey *(29)*.

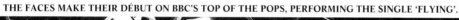
THE FACES MAKE THEIR DÉBUT ON BBC'S TOP OF THE POPS, PERFORMING THE SINGLE 'FLYING'.

13 November
The Faces release their second single 'Had Me A Real Good Time' backed with the instrumental 'Rear Wheel Skid'. Once again, the group make an appearance on *Top Of The Pops* but the single fails to chart.

29 NOVEMBER
The Faces are on Radio 1's *John Peel Sunday Concert*.

DECEMBER
Dates: North East London Polytechnic, London *(4)*, University, Sheffield *(5)*, Black Prince Hotel *(6)*, Sisters Club, Seven Sisters, London *(12)*.

The Faces embark on tours of Germany (five days) and Switzerland (six days).

7 December
The Faces appear in a private event at London's Marquee. The performance is filmed by Germany's WDR-TV for screening in that country early in 1971.

8 December
The Faces, Marc Bolan, Robert Wyatt and Sonja Kristina (of Curved Air) record Christmas carols for the Boxing Day edition of John Peel's *Top Gear* radio show. The session is conducted by Peel's producer John Walters and also features David Bedford on piano. Rod sings 'Away In A Manger' accompanied by piano only and the session sheet for this historic occasion records that the BBC paid The Faces a £50 fee.

1971

JANUARY
Dates: City Hall, Newcastle *(20)*, Trent Polytechnic, Nottingham *(22)*, University, Bradford *(23)*, The Greyhound, Croydon *(24)*, Town Hall, Birmingham *(27)*, University, Exeter *(29)*, Westfield College, Hampstead, London *(30)*, Winter Gardens, Bournemouth *(31)*.

Three gigs are cancelled when Rod goes down with laryngitis. Gigs affected are the Nags Head *(15 Jan)*, London School of Economics *(16)* and Cheltenham Town Hall *(17)*.

FEBRUARY
Dates: Marquee *(1)*, Jersey City, NJ *(5)*, Music Hall Theater, Boston, Mass *(9)*.

5 February
The Faces begin their third tour of the US in Jersey City.

MARCH
Dates: The Forum, Inglewood, Ca *(10)*, The Roundhouse, Camden, London *(30)*.

During a week's break in The Faces' US tour, Rod flies back to London to produce one side of the album 'It Ain't Easy' for Long John Baldry. The other side is produced by Elton John.
   The Faces release the album 'Long Player'. It charts at No 31 in UK and No 29 in the US.

APRIL
Dates: Orchid Ballroom, Purley, Surrey *(11)*, University, Nottingham *(24)*, Roundhouse *(29)*, University, Lancaster *(30)*.

22 April
The Faces are featured on BBC 2's *Disco 2*. They perform 'Sweet Lady Mary', 'Tell Everyone' and 'Bad'n'Ruin'.

MAY
Dates: LSE, London *(1)*, Town Hall, Watford *(6)*, Sussex Sports Centre, Brighton *(7)*, Polytechnic, Leicester *(8)*, Nags Head, Northampton *(14)*, The Crystal Palace Bowl, London

(15), Greyhound, Croydon *(16)*, Town Hall, Birmingham *(18)*, Town Hall, Cheltenham *(20)*, University, Loughborough *(21)*, Stadium, Liverpool *(22)*, Victoria Hall, Hull *(23)*, Winter Gardens, Bournemouth *(26)*, Greyhound, Croydon *(30)*.

JULY

Dates: Friars Club, Aylesbury *(2)*, Polytechnic, Kingston *(3)*, Spectrum, Philadelphia, Pa *(9)*, Cleveland, Ohio *(10)*, Minneapolis, Minn *(11)*, Milwaukee, Wis *(14)*, Pittsburgh, Pa *(16)*, Dayton, Ohio *(17)*, Toledo, Ohio *(18)*, Chicago, Ill *(20 & 21)*, Miami, Fla *(23)*, Orlando, Fla *(24)*, New Orleans, La *(25)*, San

ROD

"'Maggie May' was a hard one to follow. The singles market is a hard market in which to sell records. With 'Maggie May' I just sat down and wrote the words to the music. I always do it that way. That was a true story, by the way, about a bird, give or take a lie or two. I hate writing words, that's the hardest part about this business as far as I'm concerned. I'm not really a natural songwriter, it's something I've brought upon myself." (*Zoo World*)

Antonio, Tx *(26)*, Houston, Tx *(28)*, Wichita, Ka *(29)*, Long Beach, Ca *(30)*, Salt Lake City, Utah *(31)*.

9 July

Rod releases his new album 'Every Picture Tells A Story'. The Faces begin their fourth US tour at The Spectrum, Philadelphia, Pennsylvania, supported by Deep Purple.

AUGUST

Dates: Bilsen Festival, Belgium *(21)*, Fillmore North, Newcastle *(27)*, Weeley Festival, Essex *(29)*.

6 August

'Reason To Believe' backed with 'Maggie May' is released as Rod's new single. DJs flip the record and 'Maggie May' becomes the A-side. It eventually reaches No 1 on both sides of the Atlantic.

29 August

The Faces and T. Rex are the star attractions at the Weeley Festival in Essex.

In the following week's *New Musical Express* Rod appears on the cover below the headline 'Weeley: A One Group Festival'. In their report

WEELEY FESTIVAL, AUGUST 29, 1971.

of the event, *NME* says: "No group generated the excitement of The Faces - fifteen minutes before they went on the crowd were clapping together empty beer cans or anything they could get their hands on in anticipation of a good set.

"'Maggie May' brought the best response of all before their closing number 'Losing You'. But the audience weren't going to let them go.

'Feel So Good' was an excellent choice of encore and it was an amazing sight to see the audience of around 100,000 all standing up and chanting back the chorus line. The Faces provided all this and more. After they'd finished my sympathies were with closing band T. Rex. After all, who could possibly follow or match the sheer brilliance of The Faces at their best."

SEPTEMBER

Dates: QE Hall, London *(5)*, The Oval, London *(18)*.

5 September

The Faces host their own sell-out concert at the prestigious Queen Elizabeth Hall in the South Bank complex, London.

18 September

At the Oval Cricket Ground in London The Faces appear second on the bill to The Who

before an audience of at least 35,000. Lindisfarne and Supertramp are also on the bill. The show is a benefit concert for victims of the famine in Bangla Desh. Rod wears a leopard skin suit and the set for the show is as follows: 'Three Button Hand Me Down', 'When Will I Be Loved', 'Maybe I'm Amazed', 'Stay With Me', 'It's All Over Now', 'Country Comfort', 'Plynth', 'Maggie May', '(I Know) I'm Losing You', 'Had Me A Real Good Time'.

ROD
"I had a few doubts about The Faces to begin with. Me and Woody used to think 'Christ, we'd better ring Jeff, this isn't going to work.' Me and Ron had come from the so-called underground then; The Faces were more pop and it was hard to match the two at first." (*RM*)

THE OVAL, LONDON, SEPTEMBER 18, 1971.

Rod is voted the best British male singer by the readers of *Melody Maker*.

October

Dates: Starkers, Bournemouth *(8)*, Kinetic Circus, Birmingham *(22)*, Free Trade Hall, Manchester *(25)*.

Rod buys Cranbourne Court near Windsor from Lord Bethel for £89,000 and moves in during early 1972. The house has 32 rooms and is surrounded by fourteen acres

ROD WITH DEE HARRINGTON, 1971.

RON WOOD
"We never foresaw the Rod thing being quite so big, everything was getting along great and then bang! It's a wonder we all survived, but I supppose we are an extraordinarily close group. We've all reached the stage now where we can co-operate within the group. There's so many people in the business who can dangle carrots under your nose, but what they can't guarantee is who you're going to have to live with and spend months on end with. Rod was incredibly good about the whole thing - you can have no idea of the amount of offers and temptations he's had. But he's got it all together and swore blind that the band is still his cup of tea."

PERFORMING 'MAGGIE MAY' ON TOP OF THE POPS, OCTOBER 1971.

of gardens with a lodge, a stable block and swimming pool. A yellow Lamborghini car sits in the drive. His girlfriend Dee Harrington moves in with him, and the couple are often seen at the Fox & Hounds pub in nearby Englefield Green where Rod's tipple is almost always a Hennessey Five Star Cognac.

7 October
Rod's single 'Maggie May' and the album 'Every Picture Tells A Story' reach No 1 in both the US and UK charts during the same week. This is the first time in chart history this extraordinary feat has ever been achieved. Rod also makes No 1 in Canada, Australia and New Zealand.

This is the dawn of Rod Stewart-mania, a period when Rod was rarely off the front pages of the weekly music press, but the downside is that Rod becomes far more popular - and sought after - than his bandmates in The Faces. At the same time, Rod's solo work attracts greater sales and praise from critics than The Faces' records.

Rod starts a series of five consecutive appearances on *Top Of The Pops*. He is backed by The Faces and disc jockey John Peel who mimes mandolin. On one show the band appear miming each other's instruments with Ron Wood on keyboards, Ronnie Lane on drums, Kenny Jones on bass and Ian McLagan on guitar. On another Rod kicks a football around the stage.

In addition to 'Every Picture Tells A Story' topping the *Billboard* Hot 100 charts, Rod's first two albums also reappear on the 200, 'Gasoline

Alley' at No 128 and 'The Rod Stewart Album' at No 168.

NOVEMBER
Dates: Fillmore, Sunderland (10), Pavilion, Bath *(13)*, St Louis, Mo *(23)*, Madison Square Garden, New York, NY *(26)*.

'(I Know) I'm Losing You' is released as the follow-up single to 'Maggie May' in the US. It reaches No 24 on the charts.

5 November
Rod is presented with five gold discs at a reception held in the Amsterdam Hilton Hotel to mark sales of 'Every Picture Tells A Story' in Germany, France, Holland, Scandinavia and the Benelux countries. He had already received a gold disc and then later a platinum disc for sales in the US. In Holland he also receives the Edison Award for being voted the Best Male Vocalist of the year.

A celebration gig, due to take place in Groningen, is cancelled when Kenny Jones falls ill.

GLYN JOHNS
"The thing that was obvious to me when I got involved with The Faces was that it was too much Rod Stewart and backing band. That wasn't necessarily anyone's fault, Rod was a success and the band weren't. I doubt if I'd work with The Faces again. Too much hoo-hah went down in the end, I made myself unpopular. I'd like to work with the band though. Rod's vocal abilities are wider than he gives himself credit for. Again he was one person I never produced, you don't produce Rod Stewart. He has a particular way of recording and it works for him." *(Sounds)*

DECEMBER
Dates: Amphitheater, Chicago, Ill *(17)*.

3 December
The Faces release the single 'Stay With Me' backed with 'Debris' as their new single. It reaches No 6 in the UK and No 17 in the US.

10 December
The Faces release their new album titled 'A Nod's As Good As A Wink To A Blind Horse' produced by Glyn Johns. It is the first time they use a producer. It reaches No 2 on the UK charts and No 6 on the US charts.

Warner Brothers withdraw all copies of 'A Nod's As Good As A Wink' so they can remove an enclosed poster which has offended many American record dealers and rack jobbers. It features hundreds of small photos, mostly in colour, taken of and by The Faces on tours, and among them are shots of groupies in various states of undress.

1972

13 January
The Faces appear on *Top Of The Pops* and perform their hit single 'Stay With Me'.

29 January
In the annual breakdown of the best selling recording artists of 1971, as compiled by the British Market Research Bureau, Rod is named as No 1 selling album artist and No 3 selling singles artist.

FEBRUARY
Dates: The Rainbow, London *(11 & 12)*.

Together with Elton John, Rod appears on *Top Of The Pops* singing back up on John Baldry's single 'Iko Iko'. Rod and Elton produced one side each of the Baldry album 'Everything Stops For Tea'.

John Baldry tells *Disc* magazine: "'Iko Iko' was off the side of my album produced by Elton and naturally enough he wanted to be part of it. Then Roddie heard and declared 'I want to be on the show too!' It was a rather hysterical moment; the first ever time that Rod Stewart and Elton John had ever met. I lie. The only time

ON STAGE WITH RONNIE 'PLONK' LANE MID 1971

they'd ever met before was some 'do' (Billy) Gaff had where people fell on the floor. Yet people seem to think that Rod Stewart and Elton John are the oldest of pals, bosom mates, musical partners for years. It's not so!"

'Handbags And Gladrags' from Rod's first album is released as a single in the US. It reaches No 42 on the charts.

9 March
Rod's first album 'The Rod Stewart Album' reaches its peak position - No 139 - on the *Billboard* charts more than two years after its initial release.

1 April
BBC2 screen a 45 minute concert of The Faces in their *Sounds For Saturday* series. The set is as follows: 'Three Button Hand Me Down', 'Maybe I'm Amazed', 'I Wanna Be Loved', 'Miss Judy's Farm', 'Love In Vain', 'Stay With Me' and '(I Know) I'm Losing You'.

21 April
The Faces headline a rock'n'roll circus tour of America from April 21 to 30, opening at the Mid-South Coliseum in Memphis and closing at the Tampa Stadium in Florida on April 30. Fleetwood Mac are special guests.

MAY
Dates: The Roundhouse, London *(6)*, Free Trade Hall, Manchester *(31)*.

JUNE
The Faces call off a proposed "mini tour" of Britain at the last moment. The group were set to play concerts at six major cities but call the tour off after the opening night at

ROD
"In my opinion, this album's much better than the last one, 'cos I don't think there's a weak track on it. I wouldn't say there's anything as great as 'Mandolin Wind', 'cos that was the best thing I've ever done. Yet there were three tracks I didn't like on 'Picture'... 'That's Alright Mama', 'Seems Like A Long Time' and 'Amazing Grace'. On this album they are all winners 'cos I came up with a new idea. I thought I'll go in with the idea that I'm making an album of singles. I had the K-Tel album in mind and I thought I'll try for an album of singles and see what happens, then fit them all together like a jigsaw when they're finished." *(NME)*

Manchester Free Trade Hall. One reason given for the cancellation is that drummer Kenny Jones' wife is expecting a baby.

JULY
Date: Nottingham Festival *(22)*.

21 July
Rod releases his fourth solo album titled 'Never A Dull Moment'. It charts at No 1 in the UK and No 2 in the US.

AUGUST
Dates: Trentham Gardens,

Stoke-on-Trent *(7)*, Reading Festival *(12)*, Cotton Bowl, Dallas, Tx *(19)*, Braves Stadium, Atlanta, Ga *(20)*, Cessna Stadium, Wichita, Ka *(21)*.

4 August
'You Wear It Well' backed with 'Lost Paraguayos' is released as Rod's new single. It reaches No 1 on the UK charts and No 13 on the US charts. Both tracks are taken from the album 'Never A Dull Moment'.

10 August
Rod is featured on *Top Of The Pops* performing 'You Wear It Well'. He is backed by The Faces, Martin Quittenton and Dick Powell.

SEPTEMBER
Date: Madison Square Garden, New York City, NY *(11)*.

26 September
After being made Tony

Blackburn's record of the week on Radio One, Python Lee Jackson's 'In A Broken Dream' enters the UK charts. Lead vocals are by Rod although he was never a member of the group and recorded the song as a session singer. The song eventually reaches No 3 on the UK charts. It had reached No 56 on the US charts four months earlier.

ROD
"It's not very good, but then I wouldn't want to stop it coming out. I was really trying to sound black. John Peel got me roped into that. He said: 'Come down and teach this guy how to sing the number.' I got in there and taught him how to sing it. I made the B-side up as I went along. It was a hype, a nick from 'Cloud Nine.' That'll tell you how old it is. I got paid for that session: my fee was two carpets for my car."

AT WEMBLEY EMPIRE POOL, OCTOBER 29, 1972.

OCTOBER

Date: Wembley Empire Pool, London *(29)*.

The Lou Reizner production of Pete Townshend's 'Tommy', featuring the London Symphony Orchestra, is released. Rod sings 'Pinball Wizard' on the album which does not chart.

10 November

'Angel', another track from 'Never A Dull Moment', backed with 'What Made Milwaukee Famous', is released as Rod's new single. It reaches No 4 on the UK charts and No 40 on the US charts.

16 November

Rod is featured on *Top Of The Pops* and performs 'Angel'. He

ROD
"What Made Milwaukee Famous' didn't make the album because it was the first song I've come up against that I didn't think I could sing. It didn't lend itself to me." (*NME*)

ROBIN NASH
(TOTP PRODUCER)
"I remember with a certain amount of horror one occasion when Ronnie Lane decided he couldn't make it. So he sent a cardboard cut-out of himself instead. It was quite amusing, but it still didn't solve the problem that we were one Face, an important Face, short!" (*Record Mirror*)

ON STAGE DURING THE 'TOMMY' ORCHESTRAL CONCERT, WITH MAGGIE BELL, DECEMBER 9, 1972.

FACES
U.K. TOUR DEC '72

1973

is backed by The Faces with the exception of Ronnie Lane who sends along a cardboard cut-out of himself.

DECEMBER
Dates: Caird Hall, Dundee *(7)*, City Hall, Newcastle *(8)*, Opera House, Blackpool *(10)*, Stadium, Liverpool *(12)*, Town Hall, Leeds *(14)*, Brixton Sundown, London *(16)*, Edmonton Sundown, London *(17 & 18)*, City Hall, Sheffield (22), Free Trade Hall, Manchester *(23)*.

9 December
Rod appears in the London stage production of Pete Townshend's rock opera 'Tommy' at the Rainbow Theatre, singing 'Pinball Wizard' which he also sang on the Lou Reizner produced orchestral album of 'Tommy'. Also appearing with the London Philharmonic Orchestra are Pete Townshend, Roger Daltrey, John Entwistle, Keith Moon, Maggie Bell, Sandy Denny and Steve Winwood.

25 December
Rod appears on the Christmas Day edition of *Top Of The Pops* and sings 'You Wear It Well'. He is backed by The Faces.

8 February
The Faces are featured on *Top Of The Pops* and perform their new single 'Cindy Incidentally'.

9 February
'Cindy Incidentally' backed with 'Skewiff (Mend The Fuse)' is released as The Faces' new single. It reaches No 2 on the UK charts and No 48 on the US charts. The A-side is a track from the forthcoming new album 'Ooh La La'.

'OOH LA LA' LAUNCH PARTY, APRIL 1973

MARCH
In the annual readers poll conducted by *Disc* magazine, Rod Stewart is voted Top Singer in both British and World sections. The Faces are voted third best band in British and World sections.

APRIL
Dates: Bristol Hippodrome *(8)*, New Theatre, Oxford *(9)*, Gaumont, Worcester *(10)*, St Paul Civic Center, St Paul, Ind *(24)*, McGraw Memorial Hall, Evanston, Ill *(26)*, Missouri Arena, St Louis, Mo *(27)*.

Rak Records re-release the B-side of Jeff Beck's 1968 single 'Love Is Blue' as the A-side. The track, 'I've Been Drinking', credited to Jeff Beck/Rod Stewart reaches No 27 on the UK charts.

1 April
BBC Paris Studios, London. A live radio broadcast by The Faces for the Radio 1 *In Concert* series.

PERFORMING 'CINDY INCIDENTALLY' ON TOP OF THE POPS, FEBRUARY 8, 1973

5 April
New Musical Express give away a free flexi single

RON WOOD
"We were all in quite a state at the time - quite a pissed state actually. Everybody was mucking about with this old blues number, so we shouted to Glyn (Glyn Johns, producer) to turn the tape on. The Stones were in the next studio and Mick and Keith came in to listen for a laugh. We thought we had to use the track somehow and the B-side for the *NME* single seemed the ideal way. It's the sort of thing we often break into at rehearsals and sessions basically to loosen up. You know, a shabby kind of backing and a sort of Jimmy Witherspoon vocal from Rod. It's a very spontaneous thing." (*NME*)

featuring extracts from The Faces' forthcoming album 'Ooh La La'. It also features a loose jam entitled 'Dishevelment Blues' specially recorded for the *NME* and not available anywhere else. The track is a send up of a twelve-bar blues.

13 April

The Faces release their fourth album titled 'Ooh La La'. It reaches No 1 on the UK charts and No 21 on the US charts.

ROD
"We're still playing the same bleedin' numbers 'cos we got nothing else to do. There's a couple of numbers on the new album. Thing is we can't play 'em.'
(*MM*)

21 April

The Faces are featured on Radio One's *In Concert* series. Recorded earlier in the month at the BBC's Paris Studios, the

RON WOOD
"'Borstal Boys' and 'Silicone Grown' could be loosely described as rave up. But I think some of the tracks aren't very identifiable as us. Like 'Flags And Banners' which Ronnie Lane sings in a very high register voice. I think the work has been spread more evenly through the band this time. It's just happened that way. I mean it's the old thing that five of us getting more involved equally does help. It takes a lot off Rod's back for a start. And it certainly is the nearest we've ever got to our stage work. I feel that with this album more than any of the others there are no 'throwaways'. Every track stands up. In fact we slung a couple off because for once we actually made more tracks than we needed - a bloody miracle."

concert is to promote the new album 'Ooh La La'. The set is as follows: 'Silicone Grown', 'Cindy Incidentally', 'Memphis', 'If I'm On The Late Side', 'My Fault', 'The Stealer', 'Borstal Boys', 'Angel', 'Stay With Me', 'True Blue', 'Twistin' The Night Away', 'Miss Judy's Farm', 'Jealous Guy' and 'Too Bad'.

In a controversial interview with *Melody Maker*'s Roy Hollingworth, Rod is critical of 'Ooh La La', much to the chagrin of the rest of The Faces. He tells Hollingworth: "It was a bloody mess. A bloody mess. But I shouldn't say that, should I? Well, I should say it in a few weeks' time. Not now. I mean, the public ain't gonna like me saying it's a bloody mess. It was a disgrace. Maybe I'm too critical. But look, I don't like it. One of the best tracks is one I don't sing on, and that's 'Ooh La La'. All that fucking about taking nine months to do an album like 'Ooh La La' doesn't prove anything. But I'm not going to say anything more about it. All right? That's it."

MAY
Dates: Boston Gardens, Boston, Mass *(2)*, Civic Center, Providence, RI *(3)*, Hampton Rhodes Coliseum,

ROD
"I've always had a weak spot for America. I think until I went there I was getting a bit paranoid about myself. When I went to America I started showing off a bit more. I came out of my shell. Five years ago in America they were a healthy audience, although I think it's healthier now than it's ever been. It's hard to say how the change in me came about, except that someone might see you and say, 'Yeah, that's pretty good', and when you're on a three month tour and you've got nothing to do but work, there are no outside interests like when you're at home.
"Looking back, I'd only listen to the last couple of solo albums I've made... nothing further back. Before that I was hung up on trying to sound black."
(*Zoo World*)

PLAYING FOOTBALL FOR CHARITY, 1973

ROD: Our new album is a disgrace ...a bloody mess

OOH LA LA

FACES ON TOUR

Hampton, Va *(5)*, Civic Center, Springfield, Mass *(7)*, Nassau Coliseum, NY *(10)*, Civic Centre, Roakoke, Va *(12)*.

26 May
Ronnie Lane announces he will leave The Faces after their London dates in June.

Ronnie tells *Sounds* magazine: "One of the reasons was that I didn't feel in control. Things just slipped from my hands. I won't ever be in somebody else's band. I doubt very much if The Faces will make another album because Rod makes his own albums and quite frankly doesn't have the time to spend on The Faces. Ron Wood seems to be cruising up everywhere. I used to have to run around and get him together to get the songs for 'Ooh La La'. That album started off with a bang then elapsed into monthly obscurity. We'd do a song, then a month later Rod would hate it and refuse to sing it. That's why I ended up singing so much on 'Ooh La La', because Rod wanted to wax the numbers. I didn't do a particularly good job because the songs weren't in my key, they were in Rod's key. So Rod turns round and slags 'Ooh La La' something awful

AT THE READING FESTIVAL, AUGUST 25 1973

in the papers and I just lost interest in the whole thing."

In an official statement, drummer Kenny Jones said: "Ronnie obviously wants to do something on his own, and there is no reason why we should stand in his way."

Ronnie Lane is eventually replaced by Japanese bassist Tetsu Yamauchi who for the past year has been playing with Free.

JUNE
Dates: Edmonton Sundown, London *(1, 3 & 4)*.

The Faces cancel a proposed tour of Europe following the collapse of drummer Kenny Jones at the Edmonton Sundown. The whole group are examined by a doctor who finds that Jones and Rod

ROD
"There's only one Ronnie and it's impossible to look for another one. The guy's a character and we'll never replace him. We're all parting on the best of terms, there's no bad feelings. I've always said Ronnie Lane is one of the best lyricists Britain's got, and he still is. He's got a great career ahead of him."

Stewart in particular are suffering from "extreme exhaustion". The tour is rescheduled for July.

June 4
This is Ronnie Lane's final appearance with The Faces. The concert is filmed and later broadcast in Europe.

JULY
The Faces tour Europe and among their dates is a German Festival where Who drummer Keith Moon is somewhat rashly invited to introduce them on stage. The dates are the first to feature new bass player Tetsu Yamauchi.

BILLY GAFF (Faces/Rod Stewart Manager):
"To me Rod Stewart will always be a great performer. I'm one hundred per cent sure he'll be singing in twenty years time simply because he can manage any sort of material." (*NME*)

AUGUST
Dates: Top Rank, Doncaster *(17)*, Reading Festival *(25)*.

Rod releases an album of old favourites, his first hits compilation, titled 'Sing It Again Rod' with a cover designed in the shape of a whisky glass. It reaches No 1 on the UK charts and No 31 on the US charts.

ROD
"'Sing It Again Rod' is selling faster than 'Never A Dull Moment'. I remixed some of the tracks, where the voice was a bit low, and I designed the sleeve. Most companies put LPs like that out without consulting the artist, but these were songs I wanted to hear again."

ROD SHOWS OFF HIS LAMBORGHINI AT CRANBOURNE COURT NEAR WINDSOR.

18 September

Rod appears on ITV's *The Russell Harty Show*. He is interviewed and sings 'Oh No Not My Baby'.

The Central London branch of the Musicians Union admits Tetsu Yamauchi when he makes his second application for a work permit.

OCTOBER

Dates: Coliseum, El Paso, Tx *(1)*, Coliseum, Denver, Co *(3)*, Coliseum, Tucson, Az *(5)*, Big Surf, Phoenix, Az *(6)*, Oakland Coliseum, Oakland, Ca *(9)*, Sports Arena, San Diego, Ca *(10)*, Long Beach Arena, Ca *(14)*, Convention Center, Anaheim, Ca *(16)*, Palladium, Los Angeles, Ca *(19)*.

'Twistin' The Night Away' from the 'Sing It Again Rod' compilation is released as a single in the US where it reaches No 59 on the charts.

NOVEMBER

Dates: East Ham, Granada *(29)*, Kilburn State Theatre *(30)*.

28 November

Rod tells John Blake of the London *Evening News* that he would like to raise funds for the Liberal Party: "I suppose if I'm honest with myself I ought to vote for the Conservatives, but I'm as sick of them as I am of the Labour Party. I didn't even think of the Liberals until I saw Jeremy Thorpe doing a phone-in programme on television and he was brilliant. I've been invited to meet up with officials of the party and I'd like to ask them what they want me to do. I might just raise money with concerts or I might do something else. It's really still early days."

17 August

This is Tetsu Yamauchi's first British appearance with The Faces.

18 August

In an incredible agreement between the Musicians Union and the Government, a complete working ban is slapped on The Faces' new bass player, Japanese Tetsu Yamauchi. The Union say he is depriving a British musician of work and the Government says it has no option but to accept the Union's recommendation.

25 August

The set for Reading was as follows: 'Miss Judy's Farm', 'Silicone Grown', 'Cindy Incidentally', 'The Stealer', 'Angel', 'True Blue', 'Stay With Me', 'I Wish It Would Rain', 'Jealous Guy', 'Borstal Boys', 'Twistin' The Night Away', 'Oh No Not My Baby' and '(I Know) I'm Losing You'.

ROD

"We're not going to back down and get anyone else. The whole matter's bloody stupid. They worry about one small Japanese bass player when there's hundreds of thousands of unemployed. They're not going to put us out of action, though. There's always the Channel Islands, for example."

BILLY GAFF

(Faces manager): "The shortsightedness of the Musicians Union has always been more than apparent. Most of their rules are antiquated and basically designed to protect musicians who have little right to call themselves musicians. Were The Faces a pit band in some London Theatre, I would agree with their ruling on Tetsu."

31 August

'Oh No Not My Baby' backed with 'Jodie' is released as Rod's new single. It reaches No 6 on the UK charts and No 59 on the US charts.

ROD

"It's a funny old single. I think if you play it too much it'll drive you barmy, but then if you play it in a year's time it won't have dated." (*Disc*)

SEPTEMBER

Dates: Omni, Atlanta, Ga *(14)*, Bay Front Center, St Petersburg, Fla *(15)*, Memorial Coliseum, Tuscaloosa, Al *(17)*, Coliseum, Richmond, Va *(20)*, Roberts Stadium, Evansville, Ind *(22)*, Coliseum, Houston, Tx *(27)*, Coliseum, San Antonio, Tx *(28)*, Moody Coliseum, Dallas, Tx *(29)*.

29 November
The Faces start their first ever full-scale nationwide UK tour at the East Ham Granada in London. The set for this tour includes the following: 'It's All Over Now', 'Too Bad - Every Picture Tells A Story', 'I'd Rather Go Blind', 'Angel', 'Maggie May', 'You Wear It Well', '(I Know) I'm Losing You', 'Stay With Me', 'I Wish It Would Rain', 'Borstal Boys', 'Twistin' The Night Away' and 'Pool Hall Richard'.

30 November
'Pool Hall Richard' backed with 'I Wish It Would Rain' is released as The Faces' new single. The B-side was recorded live at the Reading Festival. It reaches No 8 on the UK charts but is not released in the US.

DECEMBER
Dates: Hippodrome, Bristol *(2)*, Odeon, Worcester *(3)*, Odeon, Birmingham *(7)*, Queen's Hall, Leeds *(8)*, Empire, Liverpool *(9)*, Free

Trade Hall, Manchester *(11)*, Opera House, Blackpool *(12)*, Apollo, Glasgow *(15 & 16)*, Odeon, Newcastle *(17)*, Winter Gardens, Bournemouth *(19)*, Granada, Sutton, Surrey *(20)*, New Theatre, Oxford *(23)*, Edmonton Sundown, London *(24)*.

8 December
BBC 2 repeats *Sounds For Saturday* featuring The Faces which was originally broadcast on April 1, 1972.

20 December
The Faces are featured on *Top Of The Pops* and perform 'Pool Hall Richard'.

1974

JANUARY
The Faces play their first dates in Australia, New Zealand and the Far East. First stop is Auckland, New Zealand, followed by five dates in Australia, one in Hong Kong and finally two in Japan.

10 January
The Faces release the live album 'Coast To Coast, Overture And Beginners'. In a strange agreement between Warner Brothers and Mercury, the LP version is released on Mercury and the cassette on Warner Brothers. The sleeve of the album credits both Rod Stewart and The Faces. The

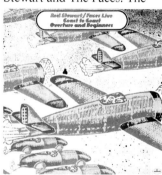

album reaches No 3 on the UK charts and No 63 on the US charts.

MAY
The Faces' record company, Warner Brothers, secure a court injunction restraining Rod from delivering the tapes of his latest solo album to Mercury. The injunction stretches until the middle of May in order to give Rod and his company, Rollgreen, time to prepare their case. The injunction restrains Rod from

KENNY JONES
"There are oldies on this album because, being live, it represents what we do on stage, but I think people will find some new life on many of the numbers. There have always been those who see us as a live band rather than a studio band, so here, within the limits of recording a live gig, is us.

"The cassette version is actually one track longer than the album for it contains 'Losing You' and it's down to recording quality why it's on one and not the other.

"Even with one track missing from the record, the playing time is just over 55 minutes and that's good value for money, for a change. Quite a bit of controversy and discussion surrounded the album's title. Rod has this idea... well you know Rod in his usual way of getting to things had walked on stage and said, 'We're going to play some music for you with four sets of fingers to one throat,' and it seemed to be interesting enough to make a title!" (*Music Scene*)

WITH ELTON JOHN AT WATFORD FOOTBALL CLUB, MAY 5, 1974.

'Mystifies Me', 'If You Gotta Make A Fool Of Somebody' and 'Take A Look At The Guy'.

AUGUST
Talking about The Faces, Rod tells *Creem* magazine: "There was a time when we didn't think people had come to listen to us, so the only way we could do it was to get pissed. God, I'd hate to think that anybody ever bought a ticket to see a Faces show because they wanted to see a bunch of drunks staggering about."

SEPTEMBER
Rod turns down offers from *Playgirl* to pose nude for $8,000 per photo. He comments: "I must admit I was a bit surprised. It's nothing of my doing, I'll tell you. I mean I'm a rampant lad and all that, hot-blooded, but some of the things they wanted me to do... I don't really think this glamorous thing is something that should be played on. I didn't do it. It all seemed so cheap and anyway, I'm not really that well endowed."

AT RON WOOD'S SOLO CONCERT, KILBURN, JULY 1974.

giving the tapes of the album to any company other than Warner Brothers.

Reports in the *NME* suggest that The Faces are about to split, and that Rod Stewart will concentrate on a solo career. Reports also suggest that Ronnie Wood is likely to form a backing band to support Stewart in his new solo career.

5 May
Rod Stewart joins Elton John on stage at Watford Football Club for a benefit concert in aid of the club.

14 June
The Faces release a maxi-single featuring 'Cindy Incidentally', 'Memphis', 'Stay With Me' and 'Pool Hall Richard'. It fails to chart.

JULY
Date: Buxton Festival *(6)*.

Rod tells *Disc* magazine that he may leave the UK for Spain, because of high taxation: "I do intend to leave the country unless there is a change of government. It's so unfair. I've worked all my life and they're going to take it all away in taxes. Anyone who has the incentive to get up and do something for themselves loses it all."

6 July
The Faces appear at the Buxton Festival, topping the bill over Humble Pie, Badger and Greenslade.

13 & 14 July
Ron Wood plays solo concerts at the Kilburn State Theatre. His band is made up of Keith Richards (guitar), Willie Weeks (bass), Ian McLagen (keyboards) and Andy Newmark (drums). Rod joins him on stage for three songs:

6 September
'I Can Feel The Fire' backed with 'Breathe On Me' is released as Ron Wood's first solo single on Warner Brothers. It fails to chart.

7 September
The Faces start a European tour at the Festival Of Cambrai in Paris. The tour continues with concerts in France, Spain, Switzerland, Germany, Belgium, Holland, Denmark, Norway and Sweden. The set for this tour is made up from the following: 'It's All Over Now', 'Take A Look At The Guy', '(I Know) I'm Losing You', 'Bring It On Home To Me/You Send Me', 'Sweet Little Rock'n'Roller', 'I'd Rather Go Blind', 'Angel', 'Stay With Me', 'You Can Make Me Dance, Sing Or Anything', 'Too Bad', 'Gasoline Alley', 'Maggie May', 'You Wear it Well', 'I Can Feel The Fire', 'Mine For Me' and 'Twistin' The Night Away'.

13 September
Ron Wood's first solo album 'I've Got My Own Album To Do' is released. Rod is featured on three songs: 'Take A Look At The Guy', 'If You Gotta Make A Fool Of Somebody' and 'Mystifies Me'. The album is not a chart success.

20 September
Rod is the guest in Radio One's *My Top 12* series hosted by Noel Edmonds. Among Rod's selection are 'Band On The Run' by Paul McCartney's Wings, 'A Change Is Gonna Come' by Sam Cooke, 'I Feel So Good' by Muddy Waters and 'Amazing Grace' by the Royal Scots Dragoon Guards.

27 September
'Farewell' backed with 'Bring It On Home To Me - You Send Me' is released as Rod's new single. It reaches No 7 on the UK charts. Both tracks are from the forthcoming album 'Smiler'. In the US 'Mine For Me' is released as a single and reaches No 91 on the charts.

4 October
Rod finally releases his new album 'Smiler' which was

held up for five months due to legal problems between Mercury Records and Warner Bros. The album enters the UK charts at No 1 and makes No 13 in the US.

Rod tells *Melody Maker*'s Chris Charlesworth in New York: "I'm very happy with 'Smiler'. There's a couple of numbers that I've done that I've always wanted to sing. 'Natural Man' is one and 'Bring It On Home To Me' is another. Paul McCartney came along to sing some numbers with me - not a bad singer either, that Paul. He says he wrote it specially for me but I don't know. It

EXCLUSIVE
JONESY GOES SOLO

FACES' drummer Kenney Jones has made a solo single. Titled *Ready or Not*, it is due for release on October 4.

It was produced by his brother-in-law Gary Osborne. Playing on the single is Gary Osborne (acoustic guitar), Mark Griffiths (bass), Jimmy McCullough from Wings (electric guitar), Peter Wood from Quiver (keyboards). Gary Osborne, Paul Vigrass and Billy Lawrie provide backing vocals. Kenney plays drums and takes lead vocals.

If the single proves to be a success, Kenney may consider recording a solo album.

"This is the first time I've ever sung on record." Kenney told *Disc*, 'so I feel quite strange about it. But I needed the challenge."

doesn't sound like a cast-off. He's mentioned something about it being for 'Red Rose Speedway', but I don't care. It's a fucking good track either way. Elton's done one for me too. Bernie said it was for me because it was a good rock'n'roll number and the only person who could sing it was me. I know for a fact that Elton wanted to record that one himself because he kept saying if I didn't want it he'd do it himself. He plays the joanna and sings it with me." Kenny Jones releases his first solo single entitled 'Ready Or Not' and backed with 'Woman Trouble'. It is not a hit.

18 October
Rod appears on the *Russell Harty Show* on London Weekend TV. He is interviewed and performs 'Farewell' and 'Bring It On Home To Me'.

NOVEMBER
Dates: Lewisham Odeon, London *(15, 17 & 18)*, Belle Vue, Manchester *(23 & 24)*, Odeon, Newcastle *(26 & 27)*, Odeon, Birmingham *(29 & 30)*.

November 18
The Faces are joined on stage by Paul and Linda McCartney who duet with Rod on 'Mine For Me'.

This date was originally scheduled for November 16th but cancelled due to Rod having problems with his throat.

BACKSTAGE AT THE LEWISHAM ODEON
WITH PAUL AND LINDA McCARTNEY, NOVEMBER 18, 1974.

22 November

'You Can Make Me Dance, Sing Or Anything' backed with 'As Long As You Tell Him' is released as the new Rod Stewart/Faces single. It reaches No 12 in the UK but fails to chart in the US.

RON WOOD

"The single really was a good step towards how we're all feeling now. It started off as about four different riffs and Rod had to come in and sew them all together with words. Eventually we just thrashed it into shape using my house as a rehearsal room. After we beat the single into shape we wrote the B-side on the spot. The single is a good direction to pursue. The guitar part didn't come till the last night. I just pretended I was Barry White's guitar player."

DECEMBER

Dates: Trentham Gardens, Stoke On Trent *(1)*, Odeon, Taunton *(3 & 4)*, Winter Gardens, Bournemouth *(6)*, New Theatre, Oxford *(8)*, Opera House, Blackpool *(10 & 11)*, Odeon, Edinburgh *(13)*, Apollo, Glasgow *(14, 16, 17 & 18)*, Kilburn State Theatre, London *(21, 22 & 23)*, Hammersmith Odeon *(24)*.

Mercury and Phonogram Records appeal against a High Court ruling that frees Rod Stewart from his contract with them. A preliminary ruling freed Rod from his Mercury contract taking effect from October 8, 1973. But the case is adjourned to allow the appeal to be heard. The case arose when Mercury was dissolved in 1972 and they assigned their Rod Stewart

ROD

"I think The Faces are a great singles band. I don't know about recording an album. I'd like us to record six or seven singles in the next six months. Obviously we wouldn't release them all. We don't work well in the studio if we're in there for long periods of time. I don't think the new single is our best. I think 'Pool Hall Richard' is." *(NME)*

contract to a new company, which in turn became Phonogram.

Rod's original contract was due to expire on October 8 1973, but under the new deal he would have been under contract to Phonogram until 1977. Rod claimed that this was done without his knowledge, and Mr Justice Willis urged that the appeal should be dealt with quickly. However, the case is further complicated when Rod challenges his contract with Warner Brothers Records who brought the action. Warner Brothers claim to have a valid contract from October 9 1973.

ROD

"The record company hassles have been a worry, I must admit. Especially as the album ('Smiler') had been finished for five months. As a matter of fact, it is a bastard. It really is. I've been treated like a motor car over the last five months. Squabbling over the product. Product is such a useless word. It's something I got myself into. It's not the record company's fault. They both have contracts, and they're both in order. As far as I'm concerned we'll just have to go to court."

14 December

Rod is met by approximately 3,000 fans when he opens Bruce's Record store in Reform Street, Dundee. The street had to be cordoned off and his car is all but overturned by the crowd.

24 December

Rod Stewart and Gary Glitter join Elton John on stage at his Hammersmith Odeon concert in London. The concert is broadcast live by BBC2's *Old Grey Whistle Test*.

UK TOUR, DECEMBER 1974.

1975

JANUARY

The Faces turn their back on the British winter for a tour of Australia, opening in Brisbane, and also playing dates in New Zealand and Japan.

4 January

In his weekly column in the British music paper *Sounds*, John Peel lists 'You Can Make Me Dance, Sing Or Anything' as his favourite single of 1974. He also places 'Farewell' at No 9.

11 January

The press report that Rod Stewart has been awarded two gold discs for his 'Smiler' album - one as producer, the other as artist - marking British sales in excess of £150,000. In fact, the sales tally had passed £500,000 when the discs were awarded.

It is announced that The Faces' British tour made the largest gross of any British tour in 1974, making over £100,000 in 24 concerts.

Ron Wood tells *Sounds* that despite constant rumours, he will not be joining The Rolling Stones: "It's funny this Rolling Stones bit cause we've never even talked about it. I suppose in another time or era I'd join the Stones. Aesthetically I'd join, because a lot of my roots and influences are there. But like I said, another time

WITH BRITT EKLAND, AT THE LONDON PRÉMIER OF THE TOMMY MOVIE, MARCH 1975.

maybe, another era. It just couldn't happen while I'm with The Faces. The Stones know that, that's why they wouldn't ask me."

The appeal by Mercury and Phonogram Records jointly against the ruling by Mr Justice Willis concerning their rights to Rod Stewart's solo albums is dismissed with costs. The effect of this is to free Rod from his contract with Mercury/Phonogram who released all his solo albums up to and including 'Smiler'. The appeal court judges ruled that Phonogram, who took over Rod's contract when Mercury was dissolved in 1972, could not extend an option on his

contract beyond the date of its expiry, and therefore have no rights to his solo recordings. Warner Brothers Records claim the rights to Rod's solo work.

FEBRUARY

Dates: Rochester, NY *(11)*, Wings Stadium, Kalamazoo, Mi *(12)*, Cobo Hall, Detroit, Mi *(14)*, Capital Center, Washington DC *(15)*, Civic Center, Philadelphia, Pa *(16)*, International Amphitheater, Chicago, Ill *(18)*, Indiana Convention Center, Indianapolis, Ind *(20)*, Civic Center, Charleston, Va *(21)*, Cincinnati Gardens, Ohio *(22)*, Madison Square Garden,

New York, NY *(24)*, Civic Center, Providence, RI *(25)*, Arena, New Haven, Ct *(26)*.

4 February

Rod attends the first night of Max Wall's one-man show at The Garrick Theatre, London.

18 February

The *Daily Mirror* reports that Rod has dated President Ford's daughter, Susan. The story makes the front page.

MARCH

Dates: Cow Palace, San Francisco, Ca *(2)*, The Forum, Los Angeles, Ca *(3 & 5)*, Swing Auditorium, San Bernadino, Ca *(7)*, Coliseum, Phoenix, Az *(9)*, HEC Edmundson Pavilion, Seattle, Wash *(12)*, PNE Coliseum, Vancouver, BC *(13)*.

1 March

Rod is featured on the pilot showing of new pop/rock TV show 'Supersonic'. He performs 'Sweet Little Rock 'n' Roller' and 'Mine For Me'.

5 March

Rod's girlfriend Dee Harrington tells the *Daily Mail*: "I don't care if we're not married as long as we're together. Obviously he gets attracted to other women sometimes and I don't mind because it keeps him in touch. But I think he knows that I'm the right one for him and that when he does get fed up I'll get him feeling better again. Whatever anyone says, I'm the one he comes home to, aren't I?"

Rod meets Swedish actress Britt Ekland, the former wife of comedian/actor Peter Sellers, at a party in Los Angeles and they embark on a highly publicised affair.

6 April

Rod flies from Heathrow Airport to Los Angeles with his new girlfriend, Britt Ekland. He tells waiting press men that he is going on a "working holiday".

15 April

Ronnie Wood announces he will join The Rolling Stones on a temporary basis and will replace Mick Taylor on the forthcoming Stones' American tour in June.

APRIL

Ian McLagan tells *Disc*: "We've started a new Faces album, but I don't know when we'll do anymore recording. Rod is into doing his own album at the moment and so is Woody. It would suit me if we started recording right now. We're very behind with recording."

Meanwhile, Rod tells

Rolling Stones get a new Face

By DEBORAH THOMAS

THE man in the dark glasses has just landed one of pop music's hottest jobs.

He is Ronnie Wood, lead guitarist with the Faces rock group — and

Now Ronnie has changed his mind.

The switch was agreed when Mick Jagger, the Stones and Faces leader Rod Stewart got together in Los Angeles.

RON WOOD

"At first I could not accept the job, because it would have meant leaving The Faces. I am too close to the whole idea of The Faces ever to turn my back on them. And I think Mick Jagger understood this as well as anybody. But finally we arrived at a formula. I will become a part-time Rolling Stone. I'll remain a full time member of The Faces and still be free to carry on with my own musical projects."

Rolling Stone: "Believe a new group album when you see it."

9 May

Rod announces he has quit Britain claiming the taxman has forced him out. Speaking from his new home in Los Angeles, he says: "Much as I love the old country, I just can't afford to live there any more. Taxation for me in Britain, at 83p in the pound, is absolutely crippling. I have lived in California a month now to see if I like it here. Well, I do. I have reluctantly made up my mind to stay, and I am applying for American citizenship. I have also told my manager to sell up everything I own in Britain."

12 May

In an interview published in *The Sun* Rod denies he has become a tax exile. He says: "These rumours that I have quit Britain for tax reasons are just not true. It's just that I am working abroad a lot, during the next few months.

My Mum would never forgive me if I quit home for good."

JUNE

Rod officially announces he has signed to Warner Brothers Records at a press conference in Burbank.

JULY

A £60,000 television show about Rod is shelved because his fast-moving way of life makes it out of date before it can get onto the screen. The documentary was made by Gaff Management who recruited chat show host, Russell Harty, to provide the commentary. The show, called *Smiler*, was filmed in Britain and America. It included concert sequences and film of Rod with Elton John in Los Angeles and singing with Paul McCartney. Billy Gaff (Rod/Faces manager): "The documentary is now out of date. We are hoping to update it so that it can be shown later."

Kenny Jones tells the *Daily Express*: "I feel pretty browned off. Ever since Rod moved to the States, everything's got disorganised. I now look on him as my friend who's gone astray." Jones says The Faces have not worked in four months and were off the road for most of 1974, and that he had lost £80,000 through their not going ahead with a series of 1975 summer football stadium concerts.

23 July

Press reports claim that Rod owes the UK taxman over £750,000. On a trip to the UK, Rod refuses to leave the international lounge to avoid being served with a tax writ.

EXIT ROD THE ROCK STAR

MILLIONAIRE pop singer Rod Stewart has quit Britain for good. He says the taxman has forced him out.

"Much as I love the old country, I just can't afford to live there any more," he said last night.

"Taxation for me in Britain, at 83p in the £, is absolutely crippling."

Rod was speaking from his new home in Beverly Hills's famous Sunset Boulevard.

The 30-year-old leader of The Faces group added: "I have lived in California a month now to see if I like it here.

"Well, I do.

"I have reluctantly made up my mind to stay, and I am applying for American citizenship.

"I have also told my manager to sell up everything I own in Britain."

This will include Rod's magnificent mansion in Windsor, Berks. It's up for sale at £300,000.

The star's manager, Billy Gaff, who is in London, said: "Britain is going to lose a lot of money-making brains and talent because of its archaic tax system.

"The country will suffer . . . it **needs** the revenue that people like Rod bring in."

Fans

Back to Rod, whose next visit to Britain will be next year, when he hopes to make a tour

By STAN SAYER

still the greatest in the world, and I am looking forward to meeting them next year."

Actress Britt Ekland, his current girl friend, said: "Rod is very unhappy about having to stay away from Britain.

29 July
The *Daily Mirror* report that a row has broken out over Ronnie Wood being on temporary loan to The Rolling Stones during their US tour. Following the extension of the Stones' tour, The Faces claim they have had to cancel three concert dates in Miami - at a loss of $20,000. A spokesman for Rod Stewart says: "We've had to cancel the concerts because there won't be enough time to rehearse new numbers with Ronnie. Rod is particularly fed up because he feels the Stones should have let him know about the extension much sooner."

AUGUST
Dates: West Palm Beach Auditorium, Fla *(15)*, Tampa, Fla *(16)*, The Omni, Atlanta, Ga *(17)*, Civic Center, Ashville, NC *(19)*, Scope, Norfolk, Va *(20)*, Roosevelt

Stadium, NJ *(22)*, Coliseum, Cleveland, Ohio *(23)*, Meskar Music Park, Evansville, Ind *(24)*, Kiel Auditorium, St. Louis, Mo *(26)*, Mid South Coliseum, Memphis, Tenn *(27)*, Myriad, Oklahoma City, Ok *(28)*, Anaheim Stadium, Ca (30), Balboa Stadium, San Diego, Ca *(31)*.

Rod, with Britt Ekland in tow, gives press interviews to promote 'Atlantic Crossing' and his forthcoming tour with The Faces. He tells *Creem* magazine: "I've got no idea what's going to happen to the band after this tour. I don't even know if our guitar player is still alive. I've spoken to him three times while he's been touring with the Stones, twice he was sounding really on top of the world and then the last time he sounded really down. We'll all be down in Miami in three weeks and we'll start

rehearsing and obviously there's going to be a lot of ego floating about. I want desperately to recreate what I've done on this album on stage and I'll do anything to do that, literally anything. We've already got a 15-piece orchestra touring with us which I know Mac (Ian McLagan) doesn't like. He's going to have to lump it."

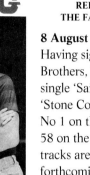

FROM THE PROMO VIDEO FOR 'SAILING'.

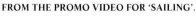

ROD
"All the songs on this album came since I left England. I didn't have a clue what I was going to do with this album. All I knew I was going to do was use Tom Dowd, and use all the musicians I'd read about. If you can't better yourself each time then there's no point in trying really. It's a solo album, made with musicians that I picked, musicians that I've always wanted to work with, the guys that worked with Otis Redding. I've got a producer that I've always wanted to use, it's got nothing to do with The Faces at all. This is the first album I've been on without Ronnie Wood. In that respect it's really a landmark for me."
(Sounds)

REHEARSING WITH THE FACES, AUGUST 1975.

8 August
Having signed with Warner Brothers, Rod releases the single 'Sailing' coupled with 'Stone Cold Sober'. It reaches No 1 on the UK charts and No 58 on the US charts. Both tracks are from the forthcoming album 'Atlantic Crossing'.

15 August
Rod releases the 'Atlantic Crossing' LP. It enters the UK charts at No 1, staying there for almost two months and makes No 9 in the US charts.

15 August
The Faces start a 40 city tour of the States at West Palm Beach Auditorium. The group is joined by guitarist Jesse Ed Davis and a twelve piece string section. The set for this tour includes the following: 'Memphis', 'It's All Over Now', 'Three Time Loser', 'Miss Judy's Farm', 'I'd Rather

Go Blind', 'Sweet Little Rock'n'Roller', '(I Know) I'm Losing You', 'Take A Look At The Guy', 'Big Bayou', 'Angel', 'Bring It On Home To Me/You Send Me', 'You Wear It Well', 'Maggie May', 'Stay With Me', 'Twistin' The Night Away', 'Smokestack Lightning'.

SEPTEMBER

Dates: Speedway, Fresno, Ca *(1)*, Spartan Stadium, San Jose, Ca *(6)*, Hughes Stadium, Sacramento, Ca *(7)*, HIC, Honolulu, Hawaii *(10 & 11)*, Coliseum, Denver, Co *(13)*, University Of New Mexico, Albuquerque, NM *(14)*, University Of Arizona, Tucson, Az *(16)*, Convention Center, San Antonio, Tx *(19)*, Hofheinz Pavilion, Houston, Tx *(20)*, Tarrant County Convention Center, Ft Worth, Tx *(21)*, Municipal Auditorium, New Orleans, La *(23)*, Municipal Auditorium, Mobil, Atlanta, Ga *(24)*, Municipal Auditorium, Nashville, Tenn *(26)*, Coliseum, Charlotte, NC *(27)*, Civic Center, Roanoke, Va *(28)*, Freedom Hall, Louisville, Ky *(30)*.

7 September
Ron Wood's brother Ted releases his début single, a version of the old Billie Holiday/Bette Midler song 'Am I Blue'. The B-side, titled 'Shine' features back up vocals by Rod Stewart, Gary Glitter and Bobby Womack.

OCTOBER

Dates: University Of Indiana, Bloomington, Ohio *(3)*, ACC South Bend, Ind *(4)*, University Of Dayton, Ohio *(5)*, Sports Arena, Toledo, Ohio *(7)*, Civic Arena, Pittsburgh, Pa *(9)*, Boston Gardens, Boston, Mass *(10)*, University Of Maryland, Baltimore, Md *(11)*, Nassau Coliseum, Uniondale, NY *(12)*, Detroit, Mi *(25)*, Hawaii *(31)*.

1 October
Al Jackson, legendary drummer with Booker T and The MGs and one of the backing musicians on 'Atlantic Crossing', is shot dead when he disturbs an intruder at his Memphis home.

NOVEMBER

Date: Hawaii *(1)*.

IAN McLAGAN
"Woody has not left the band. Jesse (Ed Davies) won't be on the British tour - and we won't have the strings either because they were a pain in the ass. We had different musicians in every town and they were never in the same key. There's not a lot we can do at the moment with Rod and Woody being out of the country. We did some recording in Nashville when we had some time. We did one old number, which we can't tell you about in case someone else nicks it, and two new songs. We had too much to think about in the middle of the tour to do any more." (*Record Mirror*)

Keen to let it be known that The Faces are still together, Ian McLagan, Kenny Jones and Tetsu Yamauchi give interviews to the music press.

7 November
'This Old Heart Of Mine' backed with 'All In The Name Of Rock'n' Roll' is released as Rod's new single. It reaches No 4 in the UK charts and No 83 in the US charts. The single marks the début of Riva Records on which all future Rod Stewart recordings will appear. Riva Records is a

IAN McLAGAN
"The thing is, Rod has chosen to state that maybe we would break up. I think people are beginning to realise that a lot of what he says in print isn't always accurate. It's a drag for the band. In America everyone came backstage looking for us to be fighting, signs of breaking up. They went out confused. People wanted us to put Rod down but our disagreements are only professional business ones. The band is more faithful to Rod than anyone he knows." (*Sounds*)

KENNY JONES
"Rod stays because he needs us and we need him. He is the singer and we're the band. We're a group called The Faces and Faces make records whenever we fucking get around to it. We will do it and it will be good." (*Sounds*)

wholly owned subsidiary of Tartan Records Limited, a new company formed earlier in the year to handle Rod's records. Legal complications prevented Tartan from using the name Rampant which was to have been the original name of the label.

BOOKER T AND THE MGS - ORGANIST BOOKER T. JONES, DRUMMER AL JACKSON, GUITARIST STEVE CROPPER AND BASSIST DONALD 'DUCK' DUNN - WHO PLAYED WITH ROD ON 'ATLANTIC CROSSING'.

WITH RONNIE WOOD ON THE FINAL FACES TOUR, AUTUMN 1975

WITH GOLD DISC FOR 'ATLANTIC CROSSING' 1975

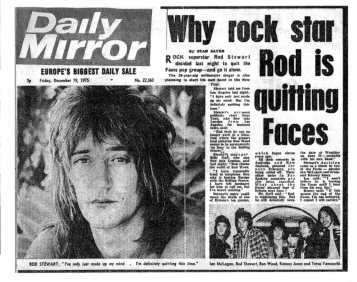

28 November
London Weekend Television screen *Rod Stewart & The Faces*, a live concert filmed at the Kilburn State Theatre on December 23, 1974. It features the following songs: 'It's All Over Now', 'Bring It On Home To Me - You Send Me', 'Sweet Little Rock'n'Roller', 'I'd Rather Go Blind', 'Angel', 'You Can Make Me Dance, Sing Or Anything', 'Twistin' The Night Away', 'You Wear It Well', 'Maggie May' and 'We'll Meet Again'.

DECEMBER
Rod's 'Atlantic Crossing' is announced as the UK's third best selling album of the year and 'Sailing' as the second best selling single.

19 December
The *Daily Mirror* is the first to report that Rod has decided to quit The Faces. The story makes the front page. *Mirror* music correspondent Stan Sayer writes: 'Rock superstar Rod Stewart decided last night to quit The Faces pop group - and go it alone. The 30-year old singer is also planning to start his own band in the New Year. Stewart told me from Los Angeles last night: "I have only just made up my mind. but I'm definitely quitting this time."

Stewart's personal publicity chief Tony Toon, who flew into London from Los Angeles for business talks, said: "Rod feels he can no longer work in a situation where the group's lead guitarist Ron Wood seems to be permanently 'on loan' to The Rolling Stones."

Stewart's manager Billy Gaff, who also flew into London, said last night: "Rod thinks the world of Ron Wood. I have repeatedly tried to telephone Ron who is touring Europe with The Rolling Stones. I have left messages for him to call me, but I've heard nothing.

"Stewart's move could mean the death of one of Britain's top groups, which began eleven years ago. All their concerts in Australia and New Zealand, planned for next February, are being called off. Their other dates in the Far Eastern countries are also being cancelled. What about The Faces planned tour of Britain next June?" Mr Gaff

said: "Rod is replanning this. But he will definitely keep the date at Wembley on June 26 - probably with his new band."

Stewart's decision came as a shock to two of the Faces - pianist Ian McLagan and drummer Kenny Jones.

Ian said: "I won't believe he is leaving The Faces until I hear it from his own lips."

Kenny said: "If this means the end of The Faces, I'm not bothered. I expect I will survive".

19 December
The London *Evening News* report that Ron Wood is to join The Rolling Stones. Mick Jagger says: "We have plans to tour Britain and the rest of Europe in March and April and we would like Ron to join us on this tour. But no contract has been finalised."

20 December
Rod tells the *Daily Mirror*: "I'd still like to work with Woody again although I'm a bit annoyed with him, the silly sod. Working with The Faces wouldn't be the same without Woody. If he wants to talk to me he can. He knows my phone number. Any of The Faces can ring me."

1976

JANUARY

British music paper *Sounds* reports that The Faces - minus Rod, but with Ron Wood - will be recording an album and are presently looking for a producer. Derek Taylor, head of Warner Brothers, tells *Sounds*: "We want them to do an album once they've found the right producer. But there's no panic. The album should not be hurried. It's important that The Faces should stay together, with or without Ron Wood." Meanwhile, Warner Brothers re-issue The Faces' first two albums as a double package entitled 'Two Originals Of'.

Tickets are put on sale for Rod's Wembley Stadium concert which is shifted from June 26 to July 3. A spokesman for The Faces denied reports that Ron Wood would be playing at the concert. He commented: "Rod has not yet worked out any plans for the concert, but in all probability he will have finalised his permanent backing outfit by that time. I am assured there is no possibility of Wood playing with Rod."

Youngblood Records release a single coupling 'The Blues' with 'Doing Fine'. The tracks, taken from the same late Sixties session which produced 'In A Broken Dream', are by Python Lee Jackson and feature Rod on lead vocal. The single fails to make the charts.

17 January

Press reports suggest that Ron Wood will be playing with Rod Stewart again - but only for one concert. Wood is said

to be one of the musicians in Rod's backing band for his concert at Wembley Stadium on June 26.

23 January

Rod is forced to postpone his British tour which was scheduled for June/July. Reason given is that there are unforeseen recording problems which would not allow sufficient time for him to form and rehearse a new band.

20 February

'It's All Over Now' backed with 'Handbags And Gladrags' is released as a single by Mercury Records.

27 February

Rod's first two albums 'An Old Raincoat Won't Ever Let You Down' and 'Gasoline Alley' are released by Mercury as a double-album package titled 'The Vintage Years 1969-70'.

9 April

'The Skye Boat Song' by The Atlantic Crossing Drum and Pipe Band is released. The single, recorded in Chicago, features bagpipes, a forty strong choir, a church organ and Rod on lead vocals. It is not a hit.

22 April

Rod gives *Rolling Stone* his first press interview since leaving The Faces to and talks about his forthcoming album and his relationship with the former Faces:

ROD, ON THE NEW ALBUM: "My new album is nearly finished. I haven't got a name for it. I haven't got a band and I doubt if I'll be touring again. I don't feel like it. I haven't used anybody from the last album, except for Steve Cropper. He did one track in Muscle Shoals. I used Tom Dowd again as producer because I think he's good. He did a good job on the last one and a better job on this one, especially with the rock'n'roll. The rock'n'roll tracks on the last album were useless. Trying to get Muscle Shoals to play rock & roll is useless.

"We put down 15 backing tracks at Cherokee Studios in Los Angeles and then got around to my singing. I couldn't hit a note. The reason, if you ask me, is the smog. It cuts the shit out of your voice. So I went to Caribou Studios (in Colorado) to put down the vocals. Nice place, but I couldn't sing there either. At 9,000 feet above sea level, you're lucky if you can walk and still breathe. The vocals were finally recorded at Miami's Criteria Sound Studios. There's a lot of my writing on this album, stuff I'm really proud of."

28 April
Rod flies into Britain with Britt Ekland for a two week promotional tour. It's his first visit to Britain for over a year due to tax reasons.

21 May
The press report that Rod has invited the Queen and Princess Margaret to a lavish party to celebrate the release of his new album.

26 May
Rod's single 'Tonight's The Night' is banned from BBC TV's *Top Of The Pops*. Rod was to have sung the song on the May 27 edition of the show, but producer Brian Whitehouse ruled that the lyrics were offensive. A spokesman for the show said:

"The record seems to be about the deflowering of a virgin. In parts it's fairly explicit."

28 May
'Tonight's The Night' backed with 'The Balltrap' is released as Rod's new single. Despite being banned by the BBC, it reaches No 5 on the UK charts. Both tracks are taken from the forthcoming album 'A Night On The Town'.

8 June
Rod holds a star studded party at Searcy's in London to celebrate the release of his new album. Guests include Marc Bolan, David Essex, Kenny Jones, Twiggy and Jonathan King.

18 June
Rod releases his new album 'A Night On The Town'. It reaches No 1 on the UK charts and No 2 on the US charts.

6 August
'The Killing Of Georgie' backed with 'Fool For You' is released as Rod's new single. Both are tracks from 'A Night

WITH A PLATINUM DISC FOR SALES OF 'A NIGHT ON THE TOWN', PRESENTED AT SEARCY'S, LONDON, JUNE 8, 1976.

On The Town'. It reaches No 2 on the UK charts.

7 August
Rod is featured in a BBC 1 television special called *Sounds Of Scotland*. He sings 'Tonight's The Night', 'Wild Side Of Life' and 'Sailing' on which he is backed by the 120 piece BBC Scottish Radio Orchestra and a choir.

31 August
Riva Records and Gaff Management move from their London office at 90 Wardour Street to new premises at 2 New King's Road.

26 September

BBC2 screen a documentary about Rod in their *Lively Arts* series. Titled *Rod The Mod Has Come Of Age - A Profile Of Rod Stewart*, it was filmed during a promotional visit to Britain and Europe during May.

Mark Kidel (producer): "Rod's style of life, sealed off from normal day-to-day problems, cannot make it easier for him to experience reality, and this may partly explain the tantrums, the frequent changes of mind and last minute cancellations. When Rod is difficult, leaving Eamonn Andrews in the lurch as he did when invited to appear on the *Today* show, it is because he wants genuine attention, and to be free from

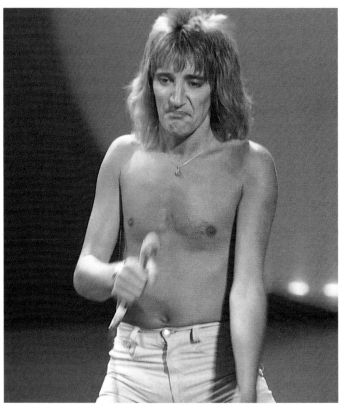

LWT SPECTACULAR 'A NIGHT ON THE TOWN', OCTOBER 1976

DEBUT SOLO TOUR, NOVEMBER 1976

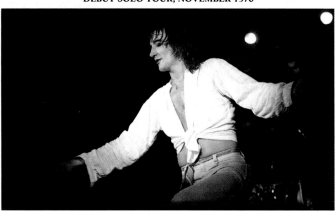

the cardboard cut-out his entourage would prefer him to be. It would be wrong to conclude that Rod does not enjoy anything in life, totally trapped by the PR operation necessary to keep him afloat. He is, after all, one of the best singers and songwriters that British rock has ever produced, and there is no doubt that he loves making music and, above all, performing in front of an audience."

OCTOBER

Rod stars in his own TV spectacular called *A Night On The Town* on London Weekend Television. Special guests are Thin Lizzy and Long John Baldry. He performs the following songs: 'Pretty Flamingo', 'The Killing Of Georgie', 'This Old Heart Of Mine', 'Wild Side Of Life', 'First Cut Is The Deepest', 'Tonight's The Night' and 'Sailing'.

New Music Express writer Roy Carr comments: "If Rod Stewart were attempting to commit artistic suicide, then he couldn't have chosen a more lethal method in front of so many people than the *A Night On The Town* special. It was cheap, it was nasty and in no way befitted an artist of Stewart's supposed stature. Aside from Lizzy's appearance, this production had absolutely nothing to commend it. I can only put it down to a shoe string production budget and a sudden, if drastic, lapse of good taste on behalf of Stewart and producer Mike Mansfield."

ROD

"It's a sign of the times. I can't go on being the same old Rod year in and year out. That's the way I felt at the time. What can you do without a band? It's very difficult without having anybody to bounce off. Look, I was on my own. What is the option - not do any TV? Then everyone says, 'Oh, fucking hell, he's not even on TV... too good to be on TV.' I can't win any more. I can't do a bloody thing right." (*Sounds*)

NOVEMBER

Dates: Trondheim, Norway *(1)*, Konsert Konsert-Pallet, Bergen *(3)*, Ekevergshalgen, Oslo *(5)*, Scandinavium, Gothenberg *(6)*, Konserthuset, Abo *(8)*, Ishallen, Helsinki *(9)*, Konsertuset, Stockholm *(13 & 14)*, Tivoli Konsertsal, Copenhagen *(16 & 17)*, Vejlbyrisskouh, Aarhus *(18)*, Eden Hall, Amsterdam *(20)*, Belle Vue, Manchester *(26, 27 & 28)*, Odeon, Birmingham *(30)*.

1 November
Rod's first solo tour opens in Trondheim, Norway. He is backed by his newly formed permanent touring band comprising Gary Grainger (guitar), Billy Peek (guitar), Jim Cregan (guitar), Phil Chen (bass), Carmine Appice (drums) and John Jarvis (keyboards). The set for this tour is made up of the following: 'Three Time Loser', 'You Wear It Well', 'Big Bayou', 'Tonight's The Night', 'Wild Side Of Life', 'This Old Heart Of Mine', 'Sweet Little Rock'n'Roller', 'The Killing Of Georgie', 'I Don't Want To Talk About It', 'Maggie May', 'Angel', 'True Blue', 'You Keep Me Hanging On', 'Get Back', '(I Know) I'm Losing You', 'Sailing', 'Stay With Me' and 'Twistin' The Night Away'.

DECEMBER
Dates: Odeon, Birmingham *(1 & 2)*, Granby Hall, Leicester *(4 & 5)*, Gaumont, Southampton *(7 & 8)*, Capitol, Cardiff *(11 & 12)*, City Hall, Newcastle *(14, 15,*

17 & 18), Olympia, London *(21, 22, 23 & 24)*, Apollo, Glasgow *(30 & 31)*.

DECEMBER
Rod's new single 'Tonight's The Night' starts an eight week run at No 1 on the US charts, becoming the longest running No 1 since The Beatles' 'Hey Jude'.

12 December
Rod releases the single 'Get Back', a track from the soundtrack of the film *All This & World War II*. It is backed with 'Trade Winds' from the 'Night On The Town' album and reaches No 11 on the UK charts.

21, 22, 23, 24 December
Rod's Olympia concerts attract a star studded audience, including Paul and Linda McCartney, Denny Laine, Liberal leader David Steel, Alvin Stardust, Marc Bolan, Gary Glitter, Rick Parfitt, Susan George, Marianne Faithfull, Twiggy, columnist Marjorie Proops, Jonathan King, producer Tom

Dowd, Elton John, Lou Reizner, former Prime Minister Edward Heath, Jeff

> **ROD**
> "We mustn't knock The Faces, but in the old days I used to walk from one side of the stage to the other, and I swear to God they weren't playing in the same time. You need a change to get that magical buzz back. I want musical respect. I would dread to think that I was selling records because Britt and I were on page three of the *Evening Whatever*. I've gotten to the point where I can't let image rule my life any more. I don't want to end up a parody of myself. On that last Faces tour I went overboard and the singing became secondary to the movements. I'm embarrassed about a lot of the things that have gone on in the last two years: some of the silly pictures that have been taken; some of the silly stuff that's been written." (*Rolling Stone*)

Beck, Steve Harley, Noel Edmunds, Annie Nightingale, Leo Sayer, Adam Faith, Linda Lewis and DJ Alan Freeman. The final concert is broadcast live on BBC2's *Old Grey Whistle Test*.

Before the opening show at Olympia Rod gives Capital Radio's Roger Scott an extensive interview for his afternoon show.

> **ROD**
> "The tour got off to a terrible start. The band and I were only just getting to know each other and I thought, 'I'll show you who can drink'. For about three weeks I was staying out all night and I wasn't eating. It didn't help. Then I got sick. Well, I was existing on port and brandy and afternoon tea and toast. When we opened at Olympia I felt so bad it was almost like somebody telling me I shouldn't be there." (*Daily Mirror*)

1977

Dates: Apollo, Glasgow *(2, 3 & 4)*, Caird Hall, Dundee *(7 & 8)*, Playhouse, Edinburgh *(10 & 11)*, Olympia, London *(14 & 15)*.

4 January

Eleven members of Rod's road crew are arrested and charged with drug offences after police raid a party at the Albany Hotel in Glasgow. The raid followed several warnings about the noise. The following day, four of the roadies - including Robin Le Mesurier (son of actor John Le Mesurier) - plead guilty to possessing cannabis and are fined a total of £225.

FEBRUARY

Dates: Entertainment Centre, Perth, Australia *(8)*, Memorial Drive, Adelaide *(11)*, Myer Music Bowl, Melbourne *(14)*, Showground, Sydney *(18)*, Festival Hall, Brisbane *(21)*.

LOU REIZNER, WHO PRODUCED ROD'S FIRST TWO SOLO ALBUMS.

'First Cut Is The Deepest' is released as the follow-up single to 'Tonight's The Night' in the US. It reaches No 21 on the charts.

12 February

Rod is voted best male singer in the annual *Record Mirror* readers poll.

15 April

Rod releases a double A-side single coupling 'First Cut Is The Deepest' from the 'A Night On The Town' album with 'I Don't Want To Talk About It' from 'Atlantic Crossing'. It reaches No 1 for four weeks on the UK charts.

16 April

Writing in the *Daily Mail* Nigel Dempster reveals: "It may be a mutual interest in sailing, but I hear that Rod Stewart has a new fan in most unlikely quarters - conductor and classical buff Edward Heath. Since attending a Stewart concert recently, he has added several of Rod's LPs to his collection. Liberal leader David Steel professes to be an equally avid fan, but I feel his motives are more political."

20 April

Rod starts recording a new album at Los Angeles Burbank Studios.

29 April

A double album anthology of The Faces titled 'The Best Of The Faces' is released. It reaches No 24 on the UK charts.

13 May

An EP featuring four Faces tracks, 'Memphis', 'You Can Make Me Dance, Sing Or Anything', 'Stay With Me' and 'Cindy Incidentally', is released. The first 15,000 copies are marketed in a coloured bag, reproducing the album sleeve of 'Best Of'. It reaches No 41 on the UK charts.

JUNE

Mercury Records release 'Mandolin Wind' from 'Every Picture Tells A Story' as a single. The B-side features two tracks from 'Smiler', 'Sweet Little Rock'n'Roller' and 'Girl From The North Country'.

Drug raids, saucy lyric and riots at a party
Could it be that rock 'n' roll is as rude and dirty as your mother always said it was?

Rod Stewart's road crew on drugs charges

Daily Mail Reporter

ELEVEN members of rock star Rod Stewart's road crew have been charged with drug offences after police raided a party at a four-star hotel.

Police were called to the Albany Hotel, Glasgow, after reports of a disturbance.

The raid followed several warnings about the noise. Stewart, who was not at the party, is staying in the hotel's £48-a-night penthouse suite with his constant companion, Britt Ekland. He is appearing at Glasgow's Apollo Theatre.

Stewart's manager, Mr Tony Toon, said last night : 'Rod is furious about the whole thing. He was asleep at the time and so were his backing group. All the people involved were from the road crew'.

The 12 arrested were taken to Cranston Hill police station, but were released last night on the understanding that they appear at Glasgow Sheriff's Court today.

Last night, solicitors from London were believed to be flying to Glasgow to help brief local lawyers.

A girl secretary was charged with obstructing police.

Mercury also release a double album titled 'The Best Of Rod Stewart' featuring tracks from Rod's five original Mercury albums. It reaches No 18 on the UK charts and No 90 on the US charts.

'The Killing Of Georgie' is released as a single in the US where it reaches number 30 on the charts.

June 26

Lou Reizner who produced Rod's albums 'An Old Raincoat Won't Ever Let You Down' and 'Gasoline Alley' dies of stomach cancer aged 44.

22 August

Rod splits up with Britt Ekland.

12 September

Britt Ekland claims $12 million from Rod at Santa Monica Superior Court, Los Angeles. She wants $3 million for her services in helping promote his career, $3 million in damages for alleged fraud and deceit and $6 million in punitive damages because Rod acted with oppression, fraud and malice.

ON STAGE WITH JIM CREGAN DURING HIS DÉBUT US TOUR AS A SOLO PERFORMER, 1977.

"It was supposed to be a double album, but we had to stop because of the tour. There was no concept. A lot of the tracks reflect what I was going through at the time with Britt. In fact, I knew the title of the album before we busted up. It must have been in the back of me mind it was going to happen. The title is a straightforward statement of independence. I felt I'd been tied down for too long and I wanted to break away." (*Rolling Stone*)

UK charts and No 2 on the US charts.

ROD
"I couldn't give a shit about Britt. Well I suppose I do miss not having someone to come home to. But I think she is doing more 'missing' than I am. I didn't intend our relationship to break up but something went wrong. She got annoyed because I took someone else out when she was away. Well, I wasn't breaking the law was I? It would have been a different case if we had been married! Though I don't take Liz Treadwell out any more and I have just got someone new. A young lady of independent means." (*Daily Express*)

18 September
Rod flies into London to watch Scotland play Czechoslovakia in the World Cup.

20 September
Rod attends the funeral of his friend, rock idol Marc Bolan, at Golders Green Crematorium in North London. David Bowie is also present.

OCTOBER
Dates: New Haven, Conn *(14)*, Largo, Md *(15)*, Buffalo, NY *(17)*, Philadelphia, Pa *(19)*, Madison Square Garden, NY *(20 & 21)*, Uniondale, NY *(23 & 24)*, Providence, RI *(25)*, Pittsburgh Civic Arena, Pa *(27)*, Lexington Center,

Louisville, Ky *(29)*, Indianapolis, Ind *(30)*, Chicago, Ill *(31)*.

7 October
'You're In My Heart' backed with 'You Got A Nerve' is released as Rod's new single. It reaches No 3 on the UK charts and No 4 on the US charts. Both are tracks from the forthcoming album 'Footloose And Fancy Free'.

14 October
Rod's début solo tour of America opens in New Haven, Conn.

28 October
Rod releases a new album titled 'Footloose And Fancy Free'. It reaches No 3 on the

NOVEMBER
Dates: St. Paul, Minn *(2)*, Richfield Coliseum, Ohio *(3)*, Cobo Arena, Detroit, Mi *(5 & 6)*, Market Square Arena, Indianapolis, Ind *(7)*, Cincinnati, Ohio *(8)*, Roanoke, Va *(9)*, Charlotte, NC *(10)*, Birmingham, Al *(18)*, Atlanta, Ga *(20)*, Jacksonville, Fla *(21)*, Hollywood, Fla *(23)*, Baton Rouge, La *(25)*, Houston, Tx *(26)*, Fort Worth, Tx *(27)*, Kansas City, Mo *(29)*, Oklahoma City, Ok *(30)*.

22 November
Guitarists Gary Grainger and Jim Cregan are arrested after a party ended in a 4am riot in their hotel room at the Hilton Hotel, Lakeland, Florida.

Police said Rod was asleep in his room when the trouble broke out. Later he bailed out his two guitarists on criminal mischief charges with a $2,000 bond. Police said: "Our officers got a call to the hotel about 4am. Curtains were ripped, lights thrown through windows, carpets damaged and parts of the ceiling were pulled down."

DECEMBER

Dates: El Paso, Tx *(2)*, Denver, Co *(5)*, Activity Center, Tempe, Az *(7)*, Tucson, Az *(8)*, Los Angeles, Ca *(12, 13 & 14)*, San Francisco, Ca *(18, 19 & 20)*.

11 December

Rod wins a top award from *Billboard* magazine for his single 'Tonight's The Night'.

22 December

Rod and eight members of his entourage run riot in the first class cabin of the DC-10 flying them from Los Angeles to London. They leave the first class section scattered with food, bottles, cigarette ends and other rubbish. Seats are damaged and smeared with honey and jam, cushions ripped and music headphones torn out. Many of the seats had vomit on them and the carpets had several cigarette burns.

Rod's party were said to be drinking heavily, being noisy and running from one end of the plane to the other. One of them deliberately tipped Rod's unwanted dinner on the floor and there was abusive language used towards the cabin staff. David Horowitz, a musical arranger for Rod's band, was arrested and charged with being drunk and disorderly. Many passengers on the flight complained, describing the scene as "looking like Steptoe's yard." Rod left the plane carrying a large glass of brandy and singing his own words to an old Al Jolson song... "I'd walk a million miles for one of your legs."

31 December

Rod wins the Best Solo Male Singer award from the *Daily Mirror*.

A MERRY ROD ARRIVES AT HEATHROW ON DECEMBER 22, 1977, AFTER CAUSING HAVOC ABOARD A DC-10.

ROD

"I can't make any excuses for what happened. All I can say is we've been touring for a year, and something had to give eventually. We sat up all the way singing and drinking. We had one hell of a party. Maybe the Christmas spirit got out of hand, but nobody got hurt so why worry?"

1978

20 January

A double A-sided single is released coupling 'Hot Legs' with 'I Was Only Joking'. It reaches No 5 on the UK charts.

In America the two sides are released separately: 'Hot Legs' reaches No 28 on the charts while 'I Was Only Joking', which follows, reaches No 22.

12 February

Rod has a lucky escape when a Rolls-Royce taking him to Heathrow Airport for a Los Angeles flight bursts into flames at 70mph on the M4.

10 May

Rod flies into London with Alana Hamilton to watch the Scottish football team in the home internationals.

19 May

'Ole Ola' backed with 'I'd Walk A Million Miles' is released as Rod's new single. The single features the Scottish World Cup Football Squad and the first 10,000 copies are released in a picture cover. It reaches No 4 on the UK charts.

2 June

Rod takes refuge under a restaurant table while armed robbers stage a shoot-out with police. The attack happened in Buenos Aires while Rod - in Argentina for the World Cup finals - was dining with record company executives. One man was shot dead and another wounded in the incident.

23 July

The BBC repeat an edited version of 1976's *Rod The Mod* documentary.

ON THE 'BLONDES HAVE MORE FUN' TOUR, DECEMBER 1978.

"The first dumb question journalists, and everyone else for that matter, ask me these days is if it's true blondes have more fun. How the hell do I know? Rock'n'Roll isn't supposed to be taken seriously. Rock never changed the face of history, it's only a reflection of life. Frankly, one of the best numbers on my album is 'Scared And Scarred', a story song about a man on Death Row. Some of the more ridiculous rock critics and writers took it quite literally. It's absurd. Does Sir Laurence Olivier have to apologise for not being Richard III every time he plays the role? I think I'm getting to the point in my career where I should go back to recording other people's material like I did in the beginning. I can't win, first they complain and say `Why don't you do something new?' So I did 'Da Ya Think I'm Sexy?', which is not about me but reflects my sense of humour towards disco. Then they crucify me for going disco. What rubbish! I love dance music. I've played, performed and recorded rock songs people can dance to since I started singing 15 years ago. My disco entry, if you can call it that, wasn't a calculated move." (*Cue*)

9 September

Music Week reports that Rod is being sued in the High Court by drummer Micky Waller who claims he has not been paid in full for work done on Rod's 'Smiler' album. In a writ issued against Rod, Rollgreen Ltd and Mr Milton Marks, a director and shareholder in Rollgreen, Waller claims £6,000 alleged to be due to him.

10 November

'Da Ya Think I'm Sexy?' backed with 'Dirty Weekend' is released as Rod's new single. It reaches No 1 on both sides of the Atlantic. Both are tracks from the forthcoming album 'Blondes Have More Fun'.

17 November

Rod releases his new album titled 'Blondes Have More Fun'. It reaches No 3 in the UK and No 1 in the US. It also made No 1 in Canada, New Zealand, Sweden and Spain.

NOVEMBER

Dates: Le Pavilon, Paris *(20)*, Forêt National, Brussels *(21)*, Ahoy, Rotterdam *(22)*, Scandinavium, Gothenburg *(24)*, Icestadium, Stockholm *(25)*, Eckbergshallen, Oslo *(27)*, Falkoner, Copenhagen *(28)*.

20 November

The opening night of Rod's 'Blondes Have More Fun Tour 1978-79'. Keyboard player John Jarvis has been replaced

by Kevin Savigar and the band has been augmented by sax player Phil Kenzie.

The set for this tour includes: 'Hot Legs', 'Born Loose', 'Tonight's The Night', 'Wild Side Of Life', 'Get Back', 'You're In My Heart', 'I Don't Want To Talk About It', 'Blondes Have More Fun', 'Da Ya Think I'm Sexy?', 'If Loving You Is Wrong', 'The Killing Of Georgie', 'Maggie May', '(I Know) I'm Losing You', 'Sweet Little Rock'n'Roller', 'Sailing', 'Twistin' The Night Away', 'You Wear It Well', 'I Just Want To Make Love To You' and 'Stay With Me'.

DECEMBER

Dates: Belle Vue, Manchester *(2, 3, 5 & 6)*, Granby Hall, Leicester *(8 & 9)*, Conference Centre, Brighton *(11, 12 & 13)*, Exhibition Centre, Birmingham *(16 & 17)*, Grand Hall. Olympia, London *(21, 22, 23, 28, 29 & 30)*.

7 December

Rod makes a visit to the aircraft carrier Ark Royal and pays his last respects before the ship is scrapped. Rod's record 'Sailing' opened the BBC's series *Sailor*, about life on the aircraft carrier and huge sales resulted. Each crew member was presented with a special limited edition blue vinyl version of 'Sailing' as a souvenir of Rod's visit.

9 December

Billy Gaff tells *Music Week*: "I still don't feel that we have really made it with Rod - in fact I would say that in Europe we are only 50% there."

31 December

Rod cancels a New Year's Eve concert at the Lyceum in London. Reason given is that Rod's voice gave out after the last Olympia concert and that some of his band had flu. However, fans are annoyed when Rod is pictured in the papers at a New Year's Eve Party in London with Alana Hamilton. Several days later Rod denies the concert was cancelled because he lost his voice: "Two members of the band had food poisoning," he said.

1979

AT THE 'MUSIC FOR UNICEF' CONCERT, JANUARY 9, 1979.

JANUARY

Date: Entertainment Centre, Perth, Australia *(31)*.

Rod appears on ITV's *The Kenny Everett Show*. He performs live versions of 'Maggie May' and 'Da Ya Think I'm Sexy' with his band.

In his only music press interview to promote 'Blondes Have More Fun' Rod tells *Creem* magazine: "I'd like to take a long time to make an album. There's always a mad rush, staying up all night to get it finished for the tour. Bollocks! I've never really got what I wanted on an album. There are people who take two years to make an album now, or a year solid in the studio, and sometimes perhaps I reckon that is the best way to do it. Because you're talking about selling nine, ten, fifteen million albums these days, and The Eagles have apparently spent a year in the studio and got twenty odd tracks, and they'll put out ten of the best ones and I'll bet they're incredible. Whereas I'll release an album feeling that I could've done it better if I'd had more time. Well, that's all going to change after this album. I'm going to take the time I want instead of trying to tour the whole world."

9 January

The 'Music For UNICEF' concert, marking the International Year Of The Child, takes place at the General Assembly Hall of the United Nations in New York. Rod sings 'Me and Bobby

McGee' with Kris Kristofferson and 'Da Ya Think I'm Sexy?'. The royalties from 'Da Ya Think I'm Sexy?' and 'Maggie May' are donated to UNICEF.

26 January
Rod issues a writ against his own record company, WEA Records, to try to stop them putting up the price of his 'Blondes Have More Fun' album from £4.49 to £4.99.

Rod holds his only Australian press conference of the tour at Rogues Restaurant in Sydney. Only blondes and those sporting blonde wigs are admitted.

'Ain't Love A Bitch' backed with 'Scared and Scarred' is released as Rod's new single. Both are tracks from the 'Blondes Have More Fun' album. Although it only reaches No 11 in the UK charts it earns a silver disc for sales over 250,000. In the US charts it reaches No 22.

FEBRUARY
Dates: Entertainment Centre, Perth, Australia *(1 & 2)*, Adelaide *(5)*, VFL Park, Melbourne *(9)*, RAS of NSW Showground, Sydney *(12 & 13)*, Festival Hall, Brisbane *(16, 17 & 18)*, Western Springs, Auckland *(22)*, QEII Park, Christchurch *(27)*.

MARCH
Dates: Neal S. Blaisdell Center Arena, Honolulu, Hawaii *(18, 19 & 20)*.

Scottish group Slippery Dick try to make a legal claim against Rod and his guitarist Gary Grainger claiming that 'I Was Only Joking' is close to a song they wrote called 'Paradise Found'. Riva Records say they consider the group to be out for publicity and that any suggestion that Rod had copied their song was totally denied.

A spokesman tells the

Evening News
BRITAIN'S BIGGEST EVENING SALE
01-353-6000
WEEKEND TV PAGES 10-11
LONDON: SATURDAY APRIL 7 1979   10p

Simple service at Tina Sinatra's home

ROCK STAR ROD WEDS

From DOUGLAS THOMPSON in Los Angeles
ROD STEWART, the rock star, who six weeks ago said he would be a bachelor for life, today married American actress Alana Hamilton.

And immediately afterwards the 34-year-old singer spoke of his plans for a family.

He said: "I would like a son born in Scotland. Then if he turns his mind to soccer he could play for Scotland."

The simple ceremony took place at the Hollywood home of Frank Sinatra's daughter Tina. The bride wore a white lace dress and Stewart had his hair dyed a paler shade of blond for the occasion.

The marriage follows a 13-month romance. Alana, 32, former wife of wealthy socialite and actor George Hamilton, has a four-year-old son Ashley.

The couple met at a publisher's party at a Beverly Hills restaurant and she said: "I don't think we've spent ten days apart since then.

"I hate people who assume Rod is just an insolent, egotistical womaniser. He is a wonderful man—bright,

THE LOVES IN THE LIFE OF SUPERSTAR ROD . . . Page Three

funny, sensitive and kind. This is the most fulfilling relationship with a man I have ever had."

The honeymoon for soccer-mad Stewart will be short. He is back at work on Monday when he starts an american tour.

All this week there have been rumours in Hollywood that the couple planned to marry, but the star and his permanent entourage denied any wedding plans.

After taking their marriage vows, the couple went to a party at the L'Ermitage restaurant in Hollywood.

Melody Maker: "If Rod wants to use someone else's song, as he has done occasionally in the past, he uses it and credits them. If this group continue with their allegations we will sue them for serious defamation against Rod and Gary."

APRIL
Dates: Edmonton Coliseum, Edmonton, Alberta *(12)*, Vancouver Coliseum, Vancouver, BC *(14 & 15)*, McNichols Arena, Denver, Co *(17)*, Hemisphere Arena, San Antonio, Tx *(19)*, The Summit, Houston, Tx *(21 & 22)*, Birmingham-Jefferson Civic Center, Birmingham, Alabama *(24)*, The Omni, Atlanta, Ga *(25)*, Freedom Hall, Louisville, Ky *(27)*, Market Square Arena, Indianapolis, Ind *(28)*, Riverfront Coliseum, Cincinnati, Ohio *(29)*.

6 April
Rod marries Alana Hamilton,

ex-wife of actor George Hamilton. The ceremony takes place at the Hollywood home of Frank Sinatra's daughter, Tina.

ROD
"Everybody said the wedding was sudden, but we decided on it a long time ago. It was just a matter of waiting for the right moment. I'd always thought I'd hear a bell ring in my head when I met the girl I was going to marry and it happened when I met Alana. I've always looked for a tall blonde wife. She's not into soccer yet, but she will be. I'll be taking her to see Scotland versus England next month."

ALANA
"I hate people who assume that Rod is just an insolent egotistical womaniser. It's not true. This is the most fulfilling relationship with a man I've ever had."

20 April

'Blondes Have More Fun' backed with 'Best Days Of My Life' is released as Rod's new single. It reaches No 63 on the UK charts.

MAY

Dates: The Uptown Theater, Chicago, Ill *(1 & 2)*, Richfield Coliseum, Cleveland, Ohio *(3 & 5)*, Maple Leaf Gardens, Toronto, Ontario *(6 & 7)*, Montreal Forum, Montreal, Quebec *(9)*, Cobo Arena, Detroit, Mi *(11, 12 & 13)*, Civic Arena, Pittsburgh, Penn *(29)*, Capital Center, Landover, Md *(30)*.

23 May

Rod and Alana fly into Britain from a belated honeymoon in Spain and announce they are expecting their first baby in August.

28 May

The BBC screen Part one of Rod's December 6 Manchester concert. Part two is screened on 2 June.

JUNE

Dates: Providence Civic Center, Providence, RI *(1)*, Boston Gardens, Boston, Mass *(2)*, Spectrum, Philadelphia, Pa *(4)*, Madison Square Garden, New York *(5, 7, 8 & 9)*, Kemper Arena, Kansas City, Mo *(11)*, Cow Palace, San Francisco, Ca *(15 & 17)*, San Diego Sports Arena, San Diego, Ca *(19)*, The Forum, Los Angeles, Ca *(21, 22, 24, 25, 26 & 28)*.

21 August

Rod becomes the father of a 6lb 13oz blonde daughter named Kimberley.

2 November

Rod releases the album 'Greatest Hits'. It reaches No 1 on the UK charts and No 22 on the US charts.

ROD
"Becoming a father doesn't mean I'll stop touring and working. That's my life."

7 November

In an interview published in *The Sun* to promote the 'Greatest Hits' album, Rod talks for the first time about why his doctor ordered him to give up drinking: "My liver had practically collapsed. I don't mind telling you I was scared. I mean, I could actually feel it. It was huge, like a ball. How much was I drinking? Well those stories that people can put away two bottles a day... it's just not humanly possible. I was doing about half a bottle of brandy a day. I had about four days of withdrawal symptoms when I stopped."

DECEMBER

To coincide with the release of Rod's 'Greatest Hits' album, 'I Don't Want To Talk About It' is released as a single for the first time in the US. It reaches No 46 on the charts.

8 December

Rod's drummer, Carmine Appice, tells *Musicians Only* magazine: "We're very conscious that the next album has to be great. I've given Rod about twenty songs I've done with a co-writer. He's got so much material to choose from he doesn't know what to pick. But Rod knows a hit record when he hears one. And he wants the album to be ace, which is why we're doing it at Olympic with Andy Johns. He's going to have Micky Waller play on a track or two. He's a good drummer and he needs it. I'm not greedy so why not?"

December

Rod's 'Greatest Hits' album is announced as the 11th best selling UK album of 1979.

LIVE IN THE USA, 1979.

1980

JANUARY

The top selling albums and singles of the Seventies are announced and Rod has six albums on the Top 100, more than any other artist. The albums in question are: 'Atlantic Crossing' (16), 'A Night On The Town' (52), 'Never A Dull Moment' (60), 'Footloose And Fancy Free' (84), 'Greatest Hits' (91) and 'Sing It Again Rod' (93).

1 January

The decade starts with Rod's 'Greatest Hits' album at No 1 on the UK charts.

25 February

The disagreement between Rod and an American music publisher as to who wrote 1978's 'Ole Ola' is resolved. Interworld Music group of America claimed the song was based on their 'Mulhera Brasileira'. Rod said he wrote it. Following a court case, the two sides share the royalty.

16 May

'(If Loving You Is Wrong) I Don't Want To Be Right' backed with 'Last Summer' is released as Rod's new single. It reaches No 23 on the UK charts.

4 July

Youngblood records re-release Python Lee Jackson's 'In A Broken Dream' with the royalties being donated to an unnamed charity of Rod's choice.

31 August

Rod's drummer Carmine Appice holds a drum clinic at the Venue in London and on 1 September at the Royal Exchange Theatre, Manchester.

LIVE ON THE 'FOOLISH BEHAVIOUR' TOUR, 1980.

1 September

Rod becomes a father for the second time when his wife Alana gives birth to a 5lb 5oz boy whom they name Sean. Rod dashes 1,000 miles from the Bahamas, where he is recording, to be at Alana's side.

> **ROD**
> "The first thing I'm going to do is get him a football."

OCTOBER

Dates: Stockholm Ice Stadium, Sweden *(11)*, Forum, Copenhagen *(12)*, Scandinavium, Gothenburg *(13)*, Hippodrome, Paris *(16)*, Palais des Sports, Lyons *(17)*, Sporthalle, Cologne *(19)*, C.C.H., Hamburg *(21 & 22)*, Deutschlandhalle, Berlin *(23)*, Sporthalle, Linz *(25)*, Olympiahalle, Munich *(26)*, Fahrhunderthalle, Frankfurt *(28 & 29)*, Stadthalle, Bremen *(30)*.

11 October

Rod opens a European tour at Stockholm in Sweden. The band line-up is the same as for the 1978/79 'Blondes Have More Fun' tour. The set includes the following: 'Hot Legs', 'Born Loose', 'Tonight's The Night', 'Sweet Little Rock'n'Roller', 'You're In My Heart', 'If Lovin' You Is Wrong', 'Dance With Me', 'Passion', 'Maggie May', 'Sailing', 'I Don't Want To

Apollo, Manchester *(9, 10 & 11)*, International Arena, Birmingham *(13 & 14)*, Conference Centre, Brighton *(16 & 17)*.

'My Girl' backed with 'Dance With Me' is released as Rod's new single. It reaches No 32 on the UK charts.

19 December
Commenting on Rod's latest tour, Alana Stewart tells *The Sun*: "It may be Rod's last tour in this form. But music is his love. Performing is his way of life. I wouldn't want him to give it up."

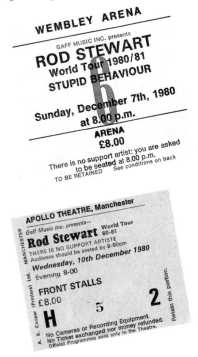

ROD
"When I was writing the song 'Foolish Behaviour' I told Alana about it and she was very understanding. She said I was just putting myself in a position that millions of husbands find themselves in. They wake up one morning with dreams of bumping off their wives and running off with a young girl to Mexico. I wrote that for all the frustrated husbands in the world, and there are plenty of them. But it's not the way I feel. I guess it was a bit of an outrageous song, but I believe that once the pen starts flowing you can't stop it." (*Daily Star*)

'Foolish Behaviour'. It reaches No 4 on the UK charts and No 12 on the US charts.

DECEMBER
Dates: Wembley Arena, London *(1, 2, 3, 5, 6 & 7)*,

Talk About It', 'Oh Carol', 'Da Ya Think I'm Sexy?', 'You Wear It Well', 'I Was Only Joking', 'Gi' Me Wings'.

31 October
'Passion' backed with 'Better Off Dead' is released as Rod's new single. It reaches No 17 on the UK charts and No 5 on the US charts. Both are tracks from the forthcoming album 'Foolish Behaviour'.

NOVEMBER
Dates: Westfalenhalle, Dortmund *(1)*, Philipshalle, Dusseldorf *(2)*, Boeblingen Stadthalle, Stuttgart *(4)*, Eissporthalle, Graz *(6)*, Stadthalle, Vienna *(7)*, Hallenstadion, Zurich *(9)*, Forêt National, Brussels *(11)*, Ahoy Halle, Rotterdam *(12)*, Dublin *(20 & 21)*, Apollo, Glasgow *(24, 25 & 26)*, Granby Hall, Leicester *(28 & 29)*.

17 November
Rod tells the *Daily Mail*: "For the first time in my life, I find that I have two personalities and that I am split right down the middle. Half of me is the family man and the other is the 35-year-old that refuses to grow up. I know deep down that it is time that I grew up. After all, you can't be in rock for the rest of your life, but I'm trapped in a business that refuses to let you grow up."

20 November
The first of Rod's two concerts in Dublin is his first ever appearance in the city. Part of the show is broadcast live from the Simonscourt Pavilion on the *Russell Harty Show* (BBC2) and Rod is interviewed for the 30 minute special.

21 November
Rod releases his new album

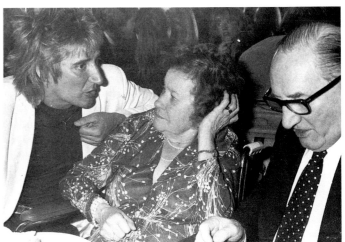

WITH PARENTS BOB AND ELSIE STEWART AT THE EMBASSY CLUB IN LONDON, DECEMBER 1980.

1981

30 January
Rod sacks band members Gary Grainger, Phil Chen and Kevin Savigar after they refuse to fly from London to L.A. to appear on the American Music Awards Show with him. Gary and Kevin claim they want to spend more time with their children.

ROD
"I can certainly appreciate what being a father means and sympathise with Gary and Kevin. But if they are working for me, it's no good if they are not with me when I need them."

FEBRUARY
Warner Home Video release Rod's first home video titled *Live At The Los Angeles Forum*.

6 March
'Oh God I Wish I Was Home Tonight' backed with 'Somebody Special' is released as Rod's new single. It is banned by the BBC and many Independent radio stations as the lyrics are considered to be suggestive. Rod says, "I think they are being a bit petty." The single fails to chart.

Meanwhile, in the US, 'Somebody Special' is released as the A-side and reaches No 71 on the charts.

APRIL/MAY
Rod tours Japan, Hong Kong and Bangkok with the new band line up, including new members Robin Le Mesurier, Danny Johnson, Jimmy Zavala and Jay Davis. Jim Cregan and Carmine Appice are kept from the old line up and Kevin Savigar rejoins after patching things up with Rod.

27 April
Prices of all Rod's UK Riva albums are slashed to around £2.99. This is to try to stop the flood of imports which are damaging UK sales.

25 May
The BBC screen an alternative version of *Rod Stewart Live At The Los Angeles Forum* with different camera shots and longer versions of the songs than those featured on the home video.

28 May
Record Mirror announce that Rod is due to release a live album featuring tracks from the European and Far East tours. A few weeks later, *The Sun* reports that it has been rejected by Warner Brothers in America due to the loud audience singing. Rod makes no comment.

OCTOBER
Rod appears on the American TV show *Saturday Night Live* and performs 'Young Turks' and a duet of 'Hot Legs' with Tina Turner. The two singers later announce plans to play live and record together.

9 October
'Tonight I'm Yours' backed

with 'Sonny' is released as Rod's new single. Both are tracks from the forthcoming album 'Tonight I'm Yours' although the B-side is advertised as being exclusive to the single. It reaches No 8 on the UK charts and No 20 on the US charts.

13 October
Rod arrives in Britain to promote his forthcoming album 'Tonight I'm Yours'.

19 October
Rod appears on the live phone-in radio show *Rockline*. It is networked across most of the US.

NOVEMBER
Dates: Greensboro Coliseum, Greensboro, SC *(11)*, Carolina Coliseum, Columbia, SC *(12)*, Louisiana Centroplex, Baton Rouge, La *(15)*, Alabama Municipal Auditorium, Mobile, Al *(16)*, Bay Front Center, St. Petersburg, Fla *(18)*,

ROD IN THE RECORDING STUDIO LISTENING TO TRACKS FROM 'TONIGHT I'M YOURS' WITH HIS ROAD MANAGER MALCOLM CULLIMORE.

Sportorium, Miami, Fla *(19)*, Memorial Coliseum, Jacksonville, Fla *(21)*, Omni, Atlanta, Ga *(22)*, Municipal Arena, Nashville, Tenn *(23 - Rod fractures his big toe at this concert)*, Capitol Center, Largo, Md *(25)*, Madison Square Garden, New York *(27)*, McNicholls Arena, Denver, Co *(30)*.

9 November

Rod releases his new album 'Tonight I'm Yours'. It reaches No 8 on the UK charts and No 11 on the US charts.

ROD

"I hope the album's as good as I think it is, because I've taken so much of a bashing over the last three or four years. I deserved a lot of the knocking that I got. I had it coming. I went through a period when I lost all contact with rock'n'roll. I was completely wound up in self image.

"My wife hates 'Tora, Tora, Tora (Out With The Boys)', absolutely detests it, because of what it stands for. And that makes me happy. Alana asks me, 'Why do you stay out drinking with the boys in the band until three in the morning after you've been in the studio with them all day?' She's got a point there. But I really think that if you're gonna' make rock'n'roll, you've got to live the lifestyle." (*Rolling Stone*)

11 November

Rod begins a four month tour of North America at the Greensboro Coliseum in North Carolina. The band consists of Wally Stoker (guitar), Jim Cregan (guitar), Robin Le Mesurier (guitar), Jay Davis (bass), Tony Brock (drums), Kevin Savigar

(keyboards) and Jimmy Zavala (harmonica/saxophone).

The set for this tour is made up of the following: 'Gi' Me Wings', 'Sweet Little Rock'n'Roller', 'Tear It Up', 'Tonight's The Night', 'Passion', 'She Won't Dance With Me'/'Little Queenie', 'Rock My Plimsoul', 'You're In My Heart', 'Hot Legs', 'Get Back', 'If Lovin' You Is Wrong', 'Tora Tora Tora (Out With The Boys)', 'Tonight I'm Yours', 'Young Turks', 'Gasoline Alley', '(I Know) I'm Losing You', 'Maggie May', 'Da Ya Think I'm Sexy', 'I Was Only Joking', 'You Wear It Well' and 'Stay With Me'.

15 November

Telling the *Sunday Mirror* of his biggest fear, Rod says: "For the first time in my career I'm really scared. I'm absolutely terrified of failure - that one day I'll make a hash of things and the fans will turn nasty. That's my biggest fear, letting down the punters."

ROD

"British journalists think I've gone on tour just to show Mick Jagger that I'm better than he is; it's a stupid comparison. You can't compete with The Rolling Stones. They're a fucking great rock'n'roll band. Out of all the concerts on the tour, there might be six where I'll be tired and feel to myself that I'm just putting it on and going through the motions, but I'm pretty inspired. To put it in a nutshell, I care. I've been at it too long not to care. It's more important to me than it ever has been, for some reason. Maybe the New Wavers gave me a kick up the ass." (*The Record*)

DECEMBER

Dates: Northlands Coliseum, Edmonton, BC *(2)*, Coliseum, Vancouver, BC *(6 & 7)*, Cow Palace, San Francisco, Ca *(9 & 10)*, Sports Arena, San Diego, Ca *(13)*, The Forum, Los Angeles, Ca *(14, 15, 18 & 19)*.

'Young Turks' backed with 'Tora Tora Tora (Out With The Boys)' is released as Rod's new single. It reaches No 11 on the UK charts and No 5 on the US charts.

19 December

This Forum concert is beamed around the world live, including the Leicester Square Odeon in London. Tina Turner and Kim Carnes make guest appearances on stage with Rod and the show attracts an estimated worldwide audience of 60 million.

WITH TINA TURNER AT THE L.A. FORUM ON DECEMBER 19, 1981.

1982

ON HOLIDAY, 1982.

'How Long' backed with 'Jealous' is released as Rod's new single. It reaches No 41 on the UK charts and No 49 on the US charts.

1 February
Rod Stewart, a book by US rock critics Paul Nelson and Lester Bangs, is published in Britain by Sidgwick and Jackson.

16 March
Rod sacks his long time manager Billy Gaff after a blazing row. The break up happens in Los Angeles towards the end of the American tour. It is reported that the pair almost came to blows during a "screaming match". The row came after months of squabbling between Rod and Gaff, allegedly over the direction of Rod's career. In a statement, Rod announces that his decision to sack Gaff is based on professional reasons and that it was amicable.

21 March
Billy Gaff makes a public plea to Rod to patch things up. In a statement he says: "I don't know what's going on in Rod's mind. He must have lost his marbles. I've been offered a fortune to write a book digging the dirt on Rod. But I don't want to kiss and tell, I want to kiss and make up. Without a manager he will be like a little boy lost."

Friends of Gaff and Rod blame Alana for the sacking. They say she has been putting pressure on Rod to switch his career from rock to MOR and even films.

11 April.
The *News Of The World* starts a four part 'exclusive' serial of stories about Rod by Tony Toon.

28 April
Rod is robbed of his £30,000 sports car - a 1977 black Porsche - by a gunman in broad daylight on Los Angeles' famous Sunset Strip. Police praise Rod for the calm way he dealt with the hold-up.

6 May
Rod is sued for £4 millon by Billy Gaff for alleged wrongful termination of their business relationship.

25 May
Rod flies into Britain and announces: "I will definitely be moving back to Britain for good. It's a bad scene in Los Angeles and it's getting worse. I don't want my kids brought up in that sort of environment. There isn't much peace in America and you are worrying all the time about robberies."

JANUARY

Dates: Dane Country Coliseum, Madison, Wis *(11)*, The Horizon, Chicago, Ill *(12)*, Reunion Area, Dallas, Tx *(14)*, The Summit, Houston, Tx *(17)*, The Richfield Coliseum, Cleveland, Ohio *(20)*, Rupp Arena, Lexington, Ky *(22)*, Joe Louis Arena, Detroit, Mi *(24)*, Civic Center, Pittsburgh, Pa *(26)*, River Front Coliseum, Cincinnati, Ohio *(28)*, Kemper Arena, Kansas City, Mo *(30)*, Checkerdome, St. Louis, Mo *(31)*.

Rod is sued for two million dollars by a film company for pulling out of a film titled 'The Killing Of Georgie'.

17 January
The *Sunday Mirror* reports that Rod and Alana have had a tiff over Britt Ekland attending a concert. Travelling back from the Californian concert, aboard a hired London style double-decker bus, Rod and Alana rowed about Britt's presence. Rod eventually stopped the bus and apparently ordered Alana off in one of the more seedy parts of Los Angeles. A cruising police car saved Alana from unwanted attention as she stood at the roadside.

FEBRUARY

Dates: Market Square Arena, Indianapolis, Ind *(1)*, Boston Gardens, Boston, Mass *(3)*, Civic Center, Providence, RI *(5)*, The Spectrum, Philadelphia, Pa *(6)*, Meadowlands, NJ *(8)*, Civic Center, Hartford, Ct *(9)*, Maple Leaf Gardens, Toronto, Ontario *(11)*, The Forum, Montreal *(14 & 15)*.

13 June
Rod and Alana hit back at recent stories in the press by giving an exclusive interview to the *Sunday Mirror*. In particular, they are upset at Tony Toon's stories about Rod which they describe as "lies and betrayal".

ROD
"Everything he wrote was either inaccurate or exaggerated. Tony always overplayed everything. Every story he put out to the press in the seven years he was working for me was exaggeration. Tony manipulated Fleet Street and I'm the first to admit he manipulated me."

ALANA
"At the outset, Tony Toon seemed determined to break us up."

26 July
A three part story by Billy Gaff titled 'The Real Rod Stewart' starts in the *Daily Star*.

AUGUST
Rod goes into the studio to mix tapes for a live album recorded on his European and US tours. He produces the album himself.

13 October
In an interview in *The Sun*, ex-Faces bass player Ronnie Lane reveals he was horrified by Rod's taste in clothes. He says: "One night Rod looked me up and down in my three piece suit and said: 'What are we trying to be tonight - a gangster?' I thought that was pretty rich coming from someone who at the time was decked out in a girl's floral blouse! I told him I'd rather look like a gangster than a go-go dancer who had gone through the change of life. We

never really spoke again after that."

24 October
The *Sunday People* track down Rod's 18-year-old illegitimate daughter, named Sarah, and arrange for her to meet Rod in Los Angeles.

6 November
Rod releases his new album 'Absolutely Live', a double live album recorded at concerts on his 1980/81 tours of America and England. It also features two previously unreleased tracks 'The Great Pretender' and 'Guess I'll Always Love You' which were recorded in the studio. It reaches No 35 on the UK charts and No 46 on the US charts.

DECEMBER
Rod records the theme song for the film 'Nightshift' titled 'That's What Friends Are For'. Although it is released as a single in a few European countries, it is only available on the sound-track album in the UK and US.
   Embassy Home Entertainment release a Rod Stewart video titled 'Tonight He's Yours', a recording of the Los Angeles Forum satellite concert from 1981.

26 December
ITV broadcast Rod's Los Angeles Forum satellite concert. It features a different selection of songs from the version released on video.

1983

ROD ON STAGE WITH HIS DAUGHTER KIMBERLEY, EUROPEAN TOUR 1983.

10 March
The Sun reports that Rod is worried about his fading popularity in Britain and this is the reason for the cancellation of a string of concerts planned for football grounds all over Britain. Instead he limits the tour to concerts in Birmingham and London.

MAY
Dates: Hall Centre Sportif, Luxembourg *(25)*, Open Air, Schuttorf (Münster) *(28)*, Forêt National, Brussels *(31)*.

9 May
Billy Gaff attacks Rod in *The Sun* saying he has become mutton dressed as lamb. The attack comes as Rod is about to start his first tour without Gaff as manager.

12 May
Elton John reveals plans for a joint tour with Rod for 1984. Elton says: "It's something

we've been planning for some time. It won't be just the two of us on stage doing an hour each. We've been working together to produce a special show which will go on tour next summer."

15 May
Rod arrives in Britain to promote his new album 'Body Wishes'.

17 May
Rod reveals that he is to receive a "seven figure sum" in compensation from Billy Gaff. Gaff is also forced to give back all Rod's publishing, TV, recording and video rights.
   Rod: "Gaff was fired strictly on the basis of his performance as my manager and business adviser."

19 May
At a press conference at the Canteen Club in London, Rod admits to being a supporter of Margaret Thatcher.

ROD

"It's a bit of a liberty for me to comment on the election as I've been away. But I think I would vote for the present Prime Minister. I think the country seems to be on the upturn and we seem to be getting out of the depression." (*Record Mirror*)

Rod also announces plans for a joint tour with Elton John in 1984.

25 May

Rod opens a three month European tour with a concert at the Hall Centre Sportif, Luxembourg. The band consists of Jim Cregan (guitar), Robin Le Mesurier (guitar), Jay Davis (bass), Tony Brock (drums), Kevin Savigar (keyboards), John Corey (keyboards/guitar), Jimmy Zavala (harmonica/ saxophone).

The set for this tour is made up of the following: 'Tonight I'm Yours', 'Sweet Little Rock'n'Roller', 'Dancin' Alone', 'Tonight's The Night', 'Passion', 'She Won't Dance With Me/Little Queenie', 'Sweet Surrender', 'I Don't Want To Talk About It', 'You're In My Heart', 'Baby Jane', 'Young Turks', 'What Am I Gonna Do?', 'Da Ya Think I'm Sexy?', 'Hot Legs', 'Gasoline Alley', 'Maggie May', 'You Wear it Well', 'I Was Only Joking', 'Sailing'.

27 May

'Baby Jane' backed with 'Ready Now' is released as Rod's new single. Both are tracks from the forthcoming album 'Body Wishes'. It reaches No 1 on the UK charts and No 14 on the US charts.

AT ROD'S SPECIAL REQUEST
EXCLUSIVELY FOR SCOTLAND

KENNEDY STREET ENTERPRISES LTD. AND HARVEY GOLDSMITH ENTERTAINMENTS
IN ASSOCIATION WITH THE DAILY RECORD AND RADIO CLYDE PRESENT

ROD STEWART
World Tour 1983
Rod's Invited Guest
GARY GLITTER
Special Guests
JOBOXERS
and Scotland's Own Passionate Friends
SATURDAY JUNE 18
IBROX STADIUM, GLASGOW
Show commences at 5pm. Doors open 3pm
Tickets £10 on the door, or £9.30 in advance (including booking fee) from

GLASGOW RANGERS F.C.   ROCKPILE RECORDS AND GROUCHO RECORDS, DUNDEE
VIRGIN RECORDS — GLASGOW.   PINK PANTHER, CARLISLE
EDINBURGH, NEWCASTLE, DURHAM.   2001, AYR
APOLLO, GLASGOW   GOLD RUSH, PERTH
H.M.V. GLASGOW   ORBIT RECORDS, FALKIRK
PLAYHOUSE AND USHER HALL, EDINBURGH.   NEW MARKET TAPES, ABERDEEN.

JUNE

Dates: Idreatsparken, Copenhagen *(3)*, Rasunda Football Stadium, Stockholm *(4)*, Congress Centrum, Hamburg *(7)*, ICC, Berlin *(8)*, Stadium Feyenoord, Rotterdam *(10)*, Stadium Mombauron, Versailles *(12)*, Palais des Sports, Paris *(13)*, La Beaujois, Nantes *(15)*, Grand Hall, Lille *(16)*, Ibrox Stadium, Glasgow *(18 - supported by Gary Glitter and Joboxers)*, RDS Pavilion, Dublin *(19 - Gary Glitter joins Rod on stage at this concert)*, NEC, Birmingham *(21, 22 & 13)*, Earls Court, London *(25, 26 & 27)*, Eisstadium, Mannheim *(29)*, Olympiahalle, Munich *(30)*.

PRESS CONFERENCE AT LONDON'S CANTEEN CLUB, MAY 19, 1983.

10 June
Rod releases his new album 'Body Wishes'. It reaches No 5 on the UK charts and No 30 on the US charts.

12 June
Simon Kinnersley takes rock journalism to new depths with an article in the *News Of The World*. Two and a half years earlier, Kinnersley had been set upon by Rod's bouncers after criticising a concert. In this article Kinnersley, with a little help from Billy Gaff, suggests Rod should retire and that his career is finished. Two weeks later, Rod performs seven highly successful British shows - all sold out - and is at No 1 on the singles chart!

IBROX STADIUM, GLASGOW, JUNE 18, 1983.

ROD
"All the ideas for this album came out after Christmas, which is only a few months back. They're all originals, all my songs. Songs from the heart. They're not silly love songs. They're positive love songs, which are always difficult for me to write - you know, admitting one's love. I don't know... it's too hard to analyse the album. I'm too close to it." (*Sounds*)

13 June
Rod speaks on French TV about the Body Wishes tour. He says: "I shall never do a tour again on this scale". He also comments on David Bowie who is on tour at the same time saying, "I don't like him. He's too arty."

19 June
Alana flies into Britain with Sean and Kimberley to watch Rod's London concerts.

25 June
Rod gives an interview to *NME*, his first for six years. Paolo Hewitt, who conducts the interview, completely distorts Rod's views, using the occasion to air his own criticisms of Rod while ignoring most of what Rod says. Over half of the two page interview contains nothing more than Hewitt's opinions of Rod.

28 June
'Baby Jane' reaches No 1 in the British charts becoming Rod's sixth No 1 single.

J U L Y
Dates: Stadio Communale, Verona *(2)*, Stadio Communale, Firenze *(3)*, Palasport, Genoa *(5)*, Velodromo Anoeta, San Sebastian *(15)*, Estadio Roman

Valero, Madrid *(17)*, Estadio Belenenses Lisboa, Lisbon *(19)*, Ramatgan Stadium, Tel Aviv *(21 & 23)*, Superbowl, Sun City, South Africa *(28, 29, 30 & 31)*.

July 2
Carol Clerk, writing in the *Melody Maker* about Rod's Earls Court concert, says: "There was nothing undignified, nothing to be ashamed of, in Rod Stewart's performance. The sound is Rock 'n' Roll, the band dynamic and he didn't put a foot wrong all night. No one could deny that this was a remarkably triumphant return."

6 July
Rod flies back to Britain after a stomach bug forces him to cancel a concert in Torino, Italy. The remaining Italian dates are also cancelled.

9 July
The letters page of the *NME* features several letters complaining about the Paolo Hewitt interview.

One is from Janet Holland, a reader from Shrewsbury, who writes: "I saw Rod Stewart at Birmingham NEC and was pleased to see he was as good as ever. Reading Paolo Hewitt's article on him, I can only suggest that he's jealous that at the age of 38 Rod's still pulling crowds. Yours was as bad as the article slagging him off in the *News Of The World*. Both talked through their arses. I conclude by quoting Rod himself: 'Thank you for putting 'Baby Jane' at number two and bollocks to the critics'."

AUGUST
Dates: Superbowl, Sun City, South Africa *(4, 5, 6 & 7)*.

Playgirl magazine ask Rod what he would do if he had only three days to live. He tells them: "I would have all my family in the studio with me. I'd like to get down a couple of tracks of my new album so I'd have something to put out when I'm dead. The last thing I would want to do would be to see Scotland put a goal past England in the World Cup - and be fucking my wife at the same time. Then I'll say 'Goodbye World!' And I'd do it blind drunk. I'd do the whole three days blind drunk. And I'd like to die in a kilt too. Buried in one. I shall speak to my lawyers about that tomorrow."

19 August
'What Am I Gonna Do' backed with 'Ghetto Blaster' is released as Rod's new single. It reaches No 3 on the UK charts and No 35 in the US.

23 August
The London *Evening News* reports that Elton John's manager John Reid is in the running to become Rod's manager.

23 August
Kenny Jones tells *The Sun* that a planned concert at the Royal Albert Hall in aid of

multiple sclerosis was born out of a drunken evening with Rod while they were discussing plans to re-form The Faces.

10 September
Rod flies in to London. *The Sun* reports him as saying he will sing at a benefit concert at the Royal Albert Hall, for Ronnie Lane, in aid of the multiple sclerosis charity on September 21.

11 September
The *News Of The World* reports that Rod and his wife Alana have separated.

12 September
Rod's mother tells the press that Rod was a "bloody fool"

to marry Alana. She added: "I could never understand why he married her in the first place. There is always an atmosphere when Alana is around. She is not a sociable sort of girl who will sit down and chat with you. In fact, she doesn't say anything at all."

13 September
Rod dismisses reports that his marriage is over as "a load of old codswallop". He says: "My marriage is under a bit of stress at the moment because I'm always touring so much. Something has to give sooner or later - but it's not going to be my marriage. I want Alana and I to stay together for the rest of our lives."

14 September

Rod talks to the *Sun* about his proposed tour with Elton John: "I've been staying down at Elton's place at Ascot for a few days and we've been working very hard. Elton and I really are getting on like a house on fire. We have found that we sing in perfect harmony. This tour really is a big project for both of us. It's taking up almost all our time. We're going to be playing lots of great material that we have never done before - lots of old Motown and soul things. I'm starting a new album next month and then after that we'll be doing the tour. I hope we'll be coming to England next February."

17 September

Press reports suggest that Rod flew back to Los Angeles with a Danish model called Christina Meyers, fuelling reports of a serious split between him and Alana.

21 September

Rod fails to perform at the charity concert for Ronnie Lane and is slammed by his fellow musicians. Many of them say that even if Rod had shown up, they would have pulled out.

> ### RONNIE LANE
> "The first I heard about Rod playing was when I read it in the papers. That was also the last I heard about it!"

Another organiser says: "Everyone is mad over this. The show is a sell out without Rod Stewart and a lot of people feel he was trying to cash in on the concert. It was a cheap stunt. He should be ashamed of himself saying he was going to appear and then just walking away."

27 September

Rod is so worried about poor sales of 'Body Wishes' in America (less than 300,000 copies) that he cancels all engagements, including his projected tour with Elton John, so he can concentrate on recording a new album.

18 November

The Sun reports that Rod and Alana are heading for a £3 million divorce. One friend says: "They both tried desperately to save the marriage, but it just won't work any more."

21 November

The *Daily Mirror*'s front page reports that Rod is spending time with American model Kelly Emberg.

23 November

Rod is pictured in the *Daily Star* and on the front cover of *The Sun* with model Kelly Emberg.

DECEMBER

Rod appears on BBC1's *Late Late Breakfast Show* via satellite from Los Angeles. He is interviewed by Noel Edmunds and performs 'Sweet Surrender'.

2 December

'Sweet Surrender' backed with 'Dancin' Alone' is released as Rod's new single. It reaches No 23 on the UK charts.

20 December

Rod flies into Britain for Christmas with his children, Sean and Kimberley. Alana joins them a few days later as they try to patch up their marriage. Rod says: "We are trying to get back together again, it is the season of goodwill."

23 December

Rod is listed as appearing on the ITV rock show *The Tube*. The appearance, apparently a recorded interview, is shelved at the last minute at Rod's request as he is captured on film with Kelly Emberg at a time when he is trying to patch things up with his wife.

30 December

Alana leaves Britain after a Christmas reunion with Rod. She says: "Right now, it's up to Rod. He has to decide if he wants to be a man with a wife and kids or a free wheeling bachelor. If he wants to go back to his old ways, then all power to him. It's just a shame he didn't decide before he had kids."

1984

15 January

Alana Stewart admits to the *Sunday Mirror* that her marriage to Rod is over: "To all intents and purposes it finished in September. Rod has lost a wife and two kids. All I have lost is someone who can't grow up. If he wants to go out with a series of young morons rather than being with me and the children I don't think I'm losing anything. I think he was going with other women all through our marriage. Rod is 39, turning 40. This is the 40 year old rock star syndrome."

1 February

A fancy dress company launch their Rod fancy dress at an Exhibition in London. It includes a vivid orange wig, white blouse, tartan scarf and nylon leopard skin trousers. Very few others have ever been immortalised in fancy dress.

3 Febuary

The Sun reports that Alana Stewart is dating Julio Iglesias.

6 March

Billy Gaff and Tony Toon comment on Rod's split with Alana. Toon says: "Alana didn't realise that Rod couldn't be changed. He will always have a tremendous sex drive and can manage it four or five times a day. She wanted him to go home after a concert and have a quiet dinner. He wants to be with the boys, guzzling beer and looking at girls. It was inevitable he would rebel and go back to his floozies."
Gaff added: "Alana is extremely faithful, strictly a

WITH JEFF BECK DURING THE FILMING OF THE 'INFATUATION' PROMOTIONAL VIDEO, APRIL 1984.

one-man woman. Rod will always be a playboy."

April

Jeff Beck talks to *Music* magazine about his reunion with Rod: "I went out to dinner with Rod one night, he put his arm round me and said 'Now what about this new band of ours?' and it was right in front of his band, but they all seemed to think it was a good idea. So to break the ice, I went over to him in the States a few weeks later to put some solos on his new album. He seems to be getting back to more raw blues based stuff, but still maintaining that up to date sound, which is what I want. We start a tour in June and it goes on for five months."

10 May

Rod flies into Britain with his girlfriend Kelly Emberg.

WITH KELLY EMBERG, 1984.

18 May

'Infatuation' backed with 1975's 'Three Time Loser' is released as Rod's new single. The A-side is from the forthcoming album 'Camouflage'. It reaches No 27 on the UK charts and No 6 on the US charts.

27 May

Rod and his girlfriend Kelly Emberg fly into Britain for the Scotland-England football match.

28 May

The BBC screen the Montreux Pop Festival and Rod is featured singing 'Infatuation' and 'Some Guys Have All The Luck'.

3 June

The League Against Cruel Sports criticise Rod for watching a bull fight in Madrid. "Someone like Rod Stewart should set a good example," said the League's executive director Richard Course.

18 June

Rod releases his new album 'Camouflage'. It reaches No 8 on the UK charts and No 18 on the US charts.

ROD

"I think there's a bit of depth to the self-penned songs that wasn't there on the last album. Those tunes were a bit shallow. This one gels together better. That's because of Michael Omartian. I felt after 'Body Wishes' - which just bombed in this country, did great in England - I was getting tired of the self producer bit. And I was looking around for a producer, heard this Donna Summer tune 'She Works Hard For The Money'. I thought, 'That's a good sounding record'. I called Michael and he agreed to do it."

ON THE NORTH AMERICAN 'CAMOUFLAGE TOUR', 1984.

JULY

Dates: Reno, Na *(3)*, Vancouver, BC *(10 & 11)*, Saddledome, Calgary *(13)*, Coliseum, Edmonton, BC *(14)*, Sacramento, Ca *(17)*, Oakland, Ca *(18)*, Pacific Amphitheater, Costa Mesa, Ca *(20 & 21)*, Phoenix, Az *(22)*, St. Louis, Mo *(26)*, Chicago, Ill *(28 & 29)*, Detroit *(31)*.

3 July

Rod starts a five month tour of North America with Jeff Beck in Reno, Nevada. He then moves on to Boise, Idaho and Portland, Oregon.

The band for this tour consists of Jim Cregan (guitar), Robin Le Mesurier (guitar), Jay Davies (bass), Tony Brock (drums), Kevin Savigar (keyboards), John Corey (keyboards/guitar), Jimmy Zavala (harmonica/saxophone), Lee Thornburg (horns) and Nick Lane (trombone).

The set is made up from a selection of the following: 'Hot Legs', 'Dance With Me', 'You Wear It Well', 'You're In My Heart', 'Tonight's The Night', 'Sweet Little Rock'n'Roller', 'Tonight I'm Yours', 'I Don't Want To Talk About It', 'Infatuation', 'Bad For You', 'Baby Jane', 'If Loving You Is Wrong', 'Hungry Heart', 'Sittin' On The Dock Of The Bay', 'Shotgun' (band only), 'Young Turks', 'Passion', 'Da Ya Think I'm Sexy', 'Maggie May', 'Some Guys Have All The Luck', 'Stay With Me' and 'We'll Meet Again.'

13 July

After only six dates, Jeff Beck leaves the tour, giving no explanation.

Rod: "I'd seen Jeff socially a few times last year. I thought to myself, 'He looks like he might have changed'. I asked him to come and play on my album, which he did. The next step was to tour together, which we did. For seven days. I think it was hard for him, because his music wasn't going down so well. This is to quote Jeff, he felt his material was a bit old-fashioned, and he was tired of doing twelve-bar blues, which is what we used to do in the Beck group. So it wasn't going down as well as we had hoped. It was great when we played 'Infatuation'. It was all right when I was on the stage with him, doing old Beck stuff. But when he was on the stage on his own, it started going downhill. I don't think he could handle it.

"We did everything to accommodate Jeff. Absolutely everything. When we first negotiated the tour, we asked about his supporting musicians. We said, 'Why don't you try the boys in the band first?' So he tried them out and said, 'They're great, I don't need any more musicians.' Then he said, 'Well, I don't want to open the act.' Obviously I said, 'Fine. You can come on in the second half of the show.' He said, 'I don't want to play "Maggie May".' I said, 'Oh, absolutely, how can you just stand there strumming an acoustic guitar?' We did everything he wanted to do, covered his demands all the way.

"It still didn't work. He knew what he was letting himself in for. He did two instrumentals that were supposed to last ten minutes, and they lasted three - 'Pump' and 'Star Cycle'. He said to the audience, 'I'll get this over with as soon as possible.' So that puts a pall on the evening. I had to come back and get it up again. I can understand it to a point. But he should have thought about that before he went on the road, before he made a commitment. You can't just run off from a tour like he did. I just wish on the day he decided not to do the tour, he'd have come out and told me. I would have understood. Would have been pissed off, but I would have understood."

JEFF BECK
"I did six shows with Rod and Calgary was the last vestige of, depths of, you know like Jeff Beck's got to leave this tour. The hand of God was pulling me out, saying don't go any further, it was stupid. The whole audience was made up of like blue-rinse Vegas type women, all sneering and leering at Rod's bum, you know, it was terrible."

20 July
'Some Guys Have All The Luck' backed with 1977's 'I Was Only Joking' is released as Rod's new single. It reaches No 15 on the UK charts and No 10 on the US charts.

27 July
Rod talks to American magazine *Bam* about his critics: "You just can't hope to make everyone happy all the time. I know damn well I'll never get a good review in *Rolling Stone*, so I don't bother to read it any more. I just know I'm not in favour any more, unlike a Bruce Springsteen who can't do anything wrong. But it's all ups and downs - I used to be their blue-eyed boy, now I'm a hopeless cause!"

AUGUST
Dates: Detroit, Mi *(2)*, Pittsburgh, Pa *(4)*, Rochester,

NY *(5)*, Binghamton, NY *(6)*, Cincinnati, Ohio *(8)*, Louisville, Ky *(10)*, Springfield, Ill *(11)*, Cleveland, Ohio *(13 & 14)*, Indianapolis, Ind *(15)*, Quebec *(17)*, Montreal *(18 & 19)*, Ottawa *(21)*, Alpine Valley, Wis *(23)*, Des Moines, Iowa *(24)*, St Paul, Minn *(25)*, Syracuse, NY *(28)*, Saratoga Springs, NY *(29)*, Canadian National Exhibition Grandstand, Toronto *(30)*.

13 August
Rod tells the press he wants to get married again and hits back at Tony Toon and Billy Gaff in *The Sun*. Of Toon he says: "I can't tell you what he did, but it was outrageous. He did the same thing twice. The first time I had him back and gave him a second chance but then he did it again and there was no way he could stay. Billy Gaff was the same, I

trusted him with my life and I was wrong."

14 August
Talking about his latest tour, Rod tells *The Sun* in England: "Nobody can accuse me of slowing up over the years. Ten years ago, when I was still with The Faces we used to go on for an hour, and I hardly moved. Now we're on stage for well over two hours and

WITH SOUL LEGEND JAMES BROWN, 1985.

I'm running about all over the place. I don't care what anyone says, I've got one of the best white soul voices in the world. No rock critic can take that away. I don't think I'll ever stop singing. I still enjoy it and feel convincing. The moment I don't is when I'll give up."

SEPTEMBER
Dates: Allentown, Pa *(1)*, Wantaugh, NY *(2)*, Madison Square Garden, New York *(10 & 11)*, Civic Center, Providence, RI *(15)*, Cumberland County Arena, Portland, Me *(16)*, Centrum, Worcester, Mass *(18)*, Capitol Center, Landover, Md *(20)*, Charleston, Va *(21)*, Knoxville, Tenn *(22)*, Civic Center, Roanoke, Va *(24)*, Coliseum, Hampton, Va *(25)*, Coliseum, Charlotte, SC *(26)*, The Omni, Atlanta, Ga *(28)*,

The Arena, Nashville, Tenn *(29)*, Von Braun Arena, Huntsville, Al *(30)*.

7 September
The *Daily Mirror* Rock and Pop Club fly 100 Rod Stewart fans out to New York to see Rod's two Madison Square Garden concerts.

OCTOBER
Dates: Coliseum, Greensboro, NC *(2)*, Coliseum, Columbia, SC *(3)*, Coliseum, Jacksonville, Fla *(5)*, Dome, Tampa, Fla *(6)*, Sportatorium, Miami, Fla *(7)*, Birmingham, Al *(11)*, New Orleans, La *(13)*, Houston, Tx *(14)*, Austin, Tx *(16)*, San Antonio, Tx *(17)*, Dallas, Tx *(19)*, Oklahoma City, Ok *(20)*, Kansas City, Mo *(21)*, Little Rock, Ark *(23)*, Albuquerque, NM *(26)*, Las Cruces, NM *(27)*, Tucson, Az *(28)*, Los Angeles, Ca *(31)*.

3 October
Rod speaks about his broken marriage: "I married the wrong person. We were miles apart. I think nine times out of ten, men have to be pushed into marriage and I was no different. The idea that I was always cheating on my wife while we were together is rubbish."

16 October
Rod's guitarist, Jim Cregan, slips on stage in Austin and splits his forehead open. He is taken by ambulance to hospital where Rod's keyboard player, Kevin Savigar, visits him with a bottle of brandy. Eventually the pair are sufficiently drunk to attract the police who arrest Savigar.

November
Dates: Los Angeles, Ca *(1)*, Las Vagas, Na *(3)*, San Diego, Ca *(4 & 5)*, Las Vegas, Na *(7)*, Oakland, Ca *(10)*, San Francisco, Ca *(11)*.

NOVEMBER
Rod undertakes a ten day tour of Japan.

22 November
Writing in *Rolling Stone*, Kelly Scott says of Rod's Atlanta concert: "The show was a fervent demonstration of what Stewart does best, with little of the Hollywood excesses that detract from his truly great singing and performing. If this tour is indicative of a re-dedication by Stewart to his rock strengths, that's the best of news."

DECEMBER
'Trouble' backed with 1981's 'Tora Tora Tora (Out With The Boys)' is released as Rod's new single in the UK. It fails to chart. In the US 'Alright Now' is released as a single. It reaches No 72 on the charts.

1985

2 January
Ron Wood marries his model girlfriend Jo Howard in London. Rod and Kelly, Jeff Beck and Peter Frampton are among the guests.

10 & 11 January
Rod appears at the Rock in Rio Festival in front of 200,000 people each night: his biggest audience ever!

FEBRUARY
Dates: Superbowl, Sun City, South Africa *(21, 22, 23, 24, 28)*.

Rod plays a controversial series of concerts in South Africa. On February 23 and March 2 there are two shows each day, one starting at 4pm, the other at 8pm, making a total of ten shows in all. During the same month Rod also tours Australia and New Zealand.

3 February
Rumours of a Faces reunion start after Rod becomes friendly with Duran Duran bassist John Taylor. The idea is put to Rod by John when they meet in a nightclub. The reformation, planned as a one off charity concert, would be in aid of the multiple sclerosis charity. Rod appears keen on the idea.

7 February
The Sun reports that Rod is taking acting lessons. Kelly is quoted as saying, "Rod only has a few years left as a rock singer. I want to make sure that he develops his acting talent so he can branch out when his recording days are over. He has shown great ability in the videos he has made, and it would be a shame to waste his acting talent."

MARCH
Dates: Superbowl, Sun City, South Africa *(1, 2 & 3)*.

4 March
Rod flies into Britain to finalise the purchase of a new home in Essex.

14 April
Reports in the press suggest that Rod's split with Alana could cost him a staggering £7 million.

MAY
Rod appears at a special concert at the Apollo Theater

AT THE APOLLO THEATER IN HARLEM, NEW YORK, MAY 1985.

ROD
"The first thing I ever did when I came to New York 17 years ago with The Jeff Beck Group was to come to the Apollo. Funnily enough, we couldn't find a taxi driver to bring us down here. Performing here is frightening because these are the guys I've looked up to all my life and copied in so many ways. It really is the highlight of my life."

WITH GEORGE MICHAEL AT ELTON JOHN'S WEMBLEY ARENA CONCERT, DECEMBER 20, 1985.

in Harlem to celebrate the re-opening of the venue. It is billed as 'Motown Returns To The Apollo'. Rod is one of only four white acts to be invited to perform, the others being Joe Cocker, Boy George and George Michael. Also on the bill are The Temptations, Diana Ross, Stevie Wonder, Wilson Pickett, Smokey Robinson, The Four Tops, Little Richard and many others. Rod performs his version of Otis Redding's 'Sittin' On the Dock Of The Bay'.

14 May
The Sun reports that Rod is arrested for drink-driving in Los Angeles. He spends three hours in a cell before being bailed out and is not charged with any offence. A police spokesman said: "It was rather strange, but Stewart was very helpful. He must have signed dozens of autographs before officers could take him away. He didn't seem concerned about being arrested or being held in a cell. He was no problem at all".

31 May
Rod and his girlfriend Kelly Emberg attend a Frankie Miller concert at the Half Moon pub in Putney, London.

24 June
Rod releases a single with Jeff Beck titled 'People Get Ready'. It reaches No 48 on the US charts. It is taken from Jeff's album 'Flash'. Neither is a hit in the UK.

11 July
The *Daily Mirror* reports that Rod has teamed up with Madonna and will be appearing at the Live Aid concert singing several duets. In the event Madonna appears alone and with the Thompson Twins but Rod does not perform at Live Aid at all.

Talking to the *Scottish Daily Record* about the event, Rod says: "I was supposed to be playing the Philadelphia show, but my guitar player couldn't get into America for the gig. By the time I found out, it was too late to rehearse with any other musicians - and I didn't want to play to backing tapes."

19 September
Rod makes an appearance at an Aids benefit concert in L.A. He duets with Cyndi Lauper singing 'People Get Ready', 'I Heard It Through The Grapevine', 'C'mon Everybody' and 'Time After Time'.

DECEMBER
Date: Tampa Stadium, Fla *(7 - a one-off date which was not part of a tour)*.

20 December
George Michael and Rod make guest appearances at Elton John's Wembley Arena concert.

1986

9 February
The British TV show *Spitting Image*, a satirical comedy show featuring unflattering puppets of celebrities and politicians, début their Rod Stewart puppet.

18 February
Rumours of a Faces reunion continue and are confirmed in the *Daily Mirror* by Kenny Jones who says: "All of us are very keen. I don't know how soon we will be going on tour but it could quite easily be any time soon."

22 April
Rod flies into Britain and announces plans for a British tour. He says: "I'm looking forward to it. We start in Belfast on June 26." He also reveals that he planned to name his new album after his father: "I wanted to call it 'Bob Stewart's son's next album' but the company turned me down on the grounds that it lacked humour."

4 May
The *News Of The World* reports that Rod has had 27 stitches in his head following an accident whilst playing football with his team, the Exiles. Apparently he collided with a member of his own team.

11 May
Rod tells the *News Of The World* that he intends to marry Kelly Emberg soon.

12 May
'Love Touch' backed with 1984's 'Heart Is On The Line' is released as Rod's new

single. 'Love Touch' is a track from the forthcoming album 'Every Beat Of My Heart'. It reaches No 27 on the UK charts and No 6 on the US charts. The 12" version is extended and also features the otherwise unavailable track 'Hard Lesson To Learn'.

Rod appears on the BBC1 chat show *Wogan* for the first time. He is interviewed and part of the video for 'Love Touch' is shown.

13 May
Rod is interviewed by Selina Scott in the first part of a two part recorded interview broadcast on TV AM. Part two is broadcast the following day.

14 May
The *Evening Standard* reports that The Faces reunion is on and that all former members have agreed to take part.

18 May
In an interview with the *News Of The World*, Rod admits that he regrets playing concerts in South Africa. He says: "I was playing to mixed audiences and anyway, music always unites people. But I must admit that I now see the importance of boycotting all businesses in and connected with South Africa. The only time I'll ever go back to South Africa will be to celebrate the end of apartheid."

19 May
Kelly Emberg flies into Britain to be with Rod while he is promoting the single 'Love Touch'.

20 May
Talking to the *Scottish Daily Record* about 1985's Live Aid concert, Rod says: "I was supposed to be playing the

Philadelphia show, but my guitar player couldn't get into America for the gig. By the time I found out, it was too late to rehearse with any other musicians - and I didn't want to play to backing tapes."

JUNE
Dates: King's Hall, Belfast *(26 & 27)*, Scottish Exhibition Centre, Glasgow *(30)*.

2 June
Rod appears on the live phone-in radio show *Rockline* which is networked across most of the US.

9 June
British newspaper *Today* reports that Nils Lofgren, the US guitarist whose most recent employer has been Bruce Springsteen, has had every track he played on expunged from Rod's new album. Rod comments: "Nils is a great guitar player but I was just trying to find the best tracks."

17 June
Rod's children Sean and Kimberley fly into Britain to stay with him for two weeks whilst Alana is on a business trip.

18 June
Radio One play Rod's new album 'Every Beat Of My Heart' for the first time. It is broacast in its entirety together with an interview with Janice Long.

20 June
Rod starts his European tour with an appearance at the Prince's Trust Charity concert at Wembley Arena. He is backed by Eric Clapton, Phil Collins, Elton John and Midge Ure (among others) and performs 'Sailing'.

23 June

Rod makes an appearance on BBC TV's *Terry Wogan Show* to promote his forthcoming single 'Every Beat Of My Heart'.

25 June

Rod releases his new album 'Every Beat Of My Heart'. It reaches No 5 on the UK charts and No 28 on the US charts where it is titled simply 'Rod Stewart'.

26 & 27 June

Rod's first European tour for three years opens with two concerts at Belfast. Band line up consists of Jim Cregan (guitar), Robin Le Mesurier (guitar), John Corey (guitar/keyboards), Charlie Harrison (bass), Tony Brock (drums), Kevin Savigar (keyboards), Jimmy Roberts (saxophone), Nick Lane (trombone) and Michael Cichowicz (trumpet).

The set for this tour is over two hours long and features a selection of the following: 'Hot Legs', 'Tonight I'm Yours', 'Tonight's The Night', 'Passion', 'Sweet Little Rock'n'Roller', 'What Am I Gonna Do', 'Dance With Me', 'Some Guys Have All The Luck', 'I Don't Want To Talk About It', 'You're In My Heart', 'Young Turks', 'In My Life', 'Infatuation', 'Sittin' On The Dock Of The Bay', 'Every Beat Of My Heart', 'Da Ya Think I'm Sexy?', 'You Wear It Well', 'Maggie May', 'Baby Jane', 'Sailing', 'Twistin' The Night Away', 'Stay With Me', '(I Know) I'm Losing You', 'Green Onions', 'In My Own Crazy Way', 'My Girl', 'Love Touch', 'The Wild Side Of Life', 'Another Heartache', 'We'll Meet Again'.

28 June

Rod Stewart attends a concert by the pop group Wham! He is accompanied by his old mate Ronnie Lane.

30 June

'Every Beat Of My Heart' backed with 1984's 'Trouble' is released as Rod's new single. It reaches No 2 on the UK charts and No 83 on the US charts.

JULY

Dates: Scottish Exhibition Centre, Glasgow *(1)*, NEC, Birmingham *(2 & 3)*, Wembley Stadium *(5)*, Hippodrome De Vincennes, Paris, France *(7)*, Merignac Stadium, Bordeaux, France *(8)*, Stade Houstoir, Lorient, France *(10)*, Westfallenhalle, Dortmund, Germany *(12)*, Schleyerhalle, Stuttgart, Germany *(13)*, Stadio Flaminio, Rome, Italy *(17)*, Velodrome Vigorelli, Milan, Italy *(19)*, Palasport, Genoa, Italy *(20)*, Plaza De Toros Monumental, Barcelona, Spain *(23)*, Rayo Vallencano FC, Madrid, Spain *(25)*, Stadium, Marbella, Spain *(27)*, Velodrome, Bilbao, Spain *(30)*.

5 July

Rod plays Wembley Stadium for the first time and despite rumours of poor ticket sales, over 66,000 people attend and it is a massive success. The Faces re-form at the end of the show for a thirty minute reunion during which they

THE RE-FORMED FACES WITH BILL WYMAN, PREPARING FOR THEIR REUNION AT WEMBLEY STADIUM.

WEMBLEY STADIUM, JULY 5, 1986.

perform 'Stay With Me', 'Twistin' The Night Away', 'Sweet Little Rock'n'Roller' and 'Losing You'. Rolling Stone Bill Wyman stands in on bass for Ronnie Lane who is crippled by multiple sclerosis.

Commenting on the bill for this Wembley Stadium concert Rod tells the *Daily Mail*: "It's

ON TOUR, 1986.

presented by Janice Long who is featured in conversation with Rod. Parts two and three are broacast on July 19 & 26 respectively.

13 July
Rumours of a split between Rod and Kelly continue as Rod is pictured in the *News Of The World* with his "new girl": 22 year old blonde Joanna Percy. Rod tells pressmen at Heathrow: "It's a load of old rubbish. There's been no great bust-up. We're still together."

AUGUST
Dates: Stade Richter, Montpelier, France *(1)*, Esplanade Du Lac, Annecy, France *(5)*, Stade De L'Ouest, Nice, France *(6)*, City Stadium, Klagenfurt,

useless. I can't stand ELO or Feargal Sharkey and I've never even heard of The Blow Monkeys. Queen have got Status Quo supporting them at Wembley. I wish I did."

7 July
Ronnie Lane hits out at Rod in the *Daily Mirror*. He claims that none of The Faces could get into the party after the Wembley Stadium show. "The security men wouldn't let us in because our names had not been left on the door," he says.

A spokesman for Rod said: "It was just one of those unfortunate things where the security let the side down."

11 July
The Sun reports that Rod has had a "bust up" with Kelly after he chose to go boozing with pals rather than stay in with her.

12 July
Radio One begins a three part series about Rod's life titled 'The Best Of Rod'. It is

AFTER A GAME OF FOOTBALL IN STOCKHOLM, AUGUST 1986.

Austria *(8)*, Airport, Ostend, Belgium *(10)*, Sporthalle, Hamburg, Germany *(12 & 13)*, Idreatsparken, Copenhagen, Denmark *(15)*, Rasunda, Stockholm, Sweden *(16)*, Budapest, Hungary *(17)*, Scandinavium, Gothenburg, Sweden *(23)*, Messehalle, Hanover, Germany *(26)*, Waldbuhne, Berlin, Germany *(28)*, Bosenbach Stadium, St. Wendel, Germany *(30)*, Patinoire Des Vernets, Geneva, Switzerland *(31)*.

8 August
The *Daily Mirror* reports that The Faces are about to embark on a world tour following their successful reunion at Wembley Stadium. Kenny Jones is reported as saying: "We will be playing absolutely everywhere, and all the money will go to Ronnie Lane's multiple sclerosis campaign. The tour should begin early next year, although Rod is trying to persuade us to start off in the Far East in November."

SEPTEMBER
Dates: Ahoy, Rotterdam, Holland *(2 & 3)*, Olympiahalle, Munich, Germany *(5)*, Hohe Warte Stadium, Vienna, Austria *(6)*, Turin, Italy *(10)*, Milan, Italy *(11)*, Verona, Italy *(12)*, NEC, Birmingham, *(15 & 16)*, Wembley Arena, London *(18 & 19)*, RDS Simonscourt, Dublin *(21 & 22)*, Wembley Arena, London *(24 & 25)*.

7 September
Rod releases a third single from the 'Every Beat Of My Heart' album: 'Another Heartache' coupled with a live version of 'You're In My Heart' from 1982's 'Absolutely Live'. It reaches

number 54 in the UK and number 52 in the US.

10 September
Rod goes ahead with a concert in Turin despite the promoter vanishing with all the ticket money. Other acts Status Quo and Ami Stewart pull out. The concert is to benefit research into AIDS.

21 September
The *Sunday Mirror* reports that Rod has been lined up for the Norman Mailer film *Tough Guys Don't Cry*.

25 September
Rod throws a party at Stringfellows in London to celebrate the huge success of his tour. Guests include George Michael, Cliff Richard, Paul Young, Gary Glitter and Ronnie Wood. Also present is Rod's ex-wife Alana. Rod is pictured with her on the front pages of many English papers

the next day. Kelly Emberg is not at the party due to modelling work commitments in Miami.

27 September
Rod cancels a concert at the Brighton Conference Centre minutes before he is due on stage. Reason given for the cancellation is a sore throat. A second Brighton concert and two Bournemouth concerts are also cancelled. All are rescheduled for November.

28 September
Rod publicly apologises to his fans for cancelling his Brighton concert at the last minute. He says: "When I tried to rehearse before the show I just could not get a note out. My voice had totally cracked. It is the first time for more than six years that I have had to cancel a show and I am bitterly upset."

OCTOBER
Dates: San Sebastian, Spain *(5)*, Madrid, Spain *(7)*, Barcelona, Spain *(9)*, Marbella, Spain *(11)*, Heidelberg, Germany *(17)*, Forêt National, Brussels, Belgium *(19)*, Palais Omnisport, Paris, France *(20)*, Frankfurt, Germany *(21)*, Bremen, Germany *(23)*, Berlin, Germany *(24)*, Kassel, Germany *(25)*, Kiel, Germany *(27)*, Düsseldorf, Germany *(28)*, Würzburg, Germany *(30)*, Stuttgart, Germany *(31)*.

Rod's keyboard player Kevin Savigar is taken seriously ill and has to pull out of the European tour. After collapsing suddenly, doctors discover a tumour in his groin. He makes a full recovery after an emergency operation and chemotherapy treatment.

25 October
Columnist/pop pundit Jonathan King attacks Rod in *The Sun*, describing him as mutton dressed as lamb, and tells him: "You've become appalling - a prancing poser."

NOVEMBER
Dates: Bournemouth International Centre, Bournemouth *(2 & 3)*, Conference Centre, Brighton *(5 & 6)*.

Rod gives an interview to the new British quality music magazine *Q* and has a rare opportunity to talk about music rather than his love life.

DECEMBER
WEA release a fourth single from the album 'Every Beat Of My Heart': a double A-side featuring 'In My Life' and 'In My Own Crazy Way'. The single fails to chart.

1987

ROD SAILS AGAIN TO AID FUND

Ferry appeal boost

By JOHN BLAKE

ROD Stewart steamed in with a fabulous boost for the Zeebrugge ferry survivors yesterday.

He plans to re-release his classic hit record Sailing and give all the profits to the disaster fund. Rod said in Los Angeles: "I was so upset about it all that I just wanted to do something.

"I watched what happened on television, then I read about it in the newspapers and it felt as though anyone I know could have been on that ship when it capsized.

"Because I am living out of the country at the moment, it was very hard to think what I could do to help those poor people.

HELPING: Rod

came the "anthem" for the Falklands Task Force in 1982.

Sailing will be backed by Every Beat of My Heart, which was a number two hit for Rod last year.

The disaster fund organisers in Dover expect the record's sales to bring in tens of thousands of pounds.

A spokesman said: "We are extremely grateful to Mr Stewart."

Sales

"I am certainly not campaigning for other stars to do things. It's just something very personal that I felt I wanted to do."

Rod topped the charts with Sailing for eleven weeks in the summer of 1975.

It went on to sell more than a million copies and again captured the na-

Have a nice day!

PRESIDENT Reagan sent birthday congratulations to 100-year-old Ann Weyman, of Ruspidge, Gloucs, who has cousins

11 March
Rod's classic single 'Sailing' is re-released (actually re-promoted, as it had never been deleted) in aid of the Zeebrugge Cross Channel Ferry Disaster Fund. It reaches No 41 in the UK charts. Boy George slams the record, saying its release is in bad taste.

22 March
The *News of The World* reports that Rod has ditched his girlfriend Kelly Emberg just two months before the birth of their child is due. He is reported to be seeing a model called Regan.

26 March
The *Daily Mirror* reports that Robin Le Mesurier has split from the Rod Stewart Band and that Jim Cregan is working with Julian Lennon.

March
Rod is featured in *The Sun* cartoon 'Striker' for several episodes.

POSING FOR SMILER MAGAZINE, AUGUST 24, 1987.

March
Rod goes into the studio to start work on a new album with ex-Duran Duran guitarist Andy Taylor.

5 April
The *News Of The World* continues its Rod/Kelly split stories with a two page article titled 'Have My Baby Then Get Out!' The article is completely made up of quotes from so-called friends of the couple.

MAY
John Taylor from Duran Duran comments on Andy Taylor's liaison with Rod in the course of a general slagging of his former Duran colleague in *Smash Hits*. He says: "I've heard he's working with Rod Stewart now - terribly desperately trendy of

him isn't it? Yes, I know I once said I was going to play with Rod Stewart but thank God I didn't."

22 May
Rod gives *Smiler*, the Stewart fanzine, an exclusive interview and reveals that he has just re-recorded 'Twistin' The Night Away' and is about to start work on a video to promote it.

> **ROD**
> "We've just re-cut 'Twistin' The Night Away' and it's bloody good. It's for the new Spielberg film called 'Innerspace'. This is the first time I've ever wanted to be really involved in a film."

24 May
Rod is invited by Scottish football club Dundee to join their board. He declines.

7 June
Rod is pictured on the front page of the *News Of The World* magazine *Sunday* with model Regan.

17 June
Rod's girlfriend Kelly Emberg gives birth to an 8lb 2oz baby daughter named Ruby.

28 June
Rod admits to the *News Of The World* that things were going wrong between him and Kelly. He says: "I've been a very silly boy. I don't know why I do these things. All I want to do is be with Kelly and Ruby. I know how much they mean to me. The trouble is I have to learn everything the hard way."

26 October
Rod releases his only new material of 1987: a new version of 'Twistin' The Night Away' from the soundtrack of the Stephen Spielberg film *Innerspace*. It reached No 80 on the US charts.

30 October
Ron Wood's art exhibition *Decades* opens in London. Among the portraits are two of Rod.

NOVEMBER
ITV screen an edited version of Rod's 1984 American San Diego concert featuring the following songs: 'Infatuation', 'Bad For You', 'Tonight's The Night', 'You're In My Heart', 'Baby Jane', Sittin' On the Dock Of The Bay', 'Young Turks', 'Passion', 'Da Ya Think I'm Sexy', 'Maggie May', 'Some Guys Have All The Luck', 'Stay With Me' and 'We'll Meet Again'.

1988

28 January
Rolling Stone reports that Rod will start a world tour in April with concerts in China. They also report that his new album is to be titled 'Pardon My Past'.

7 March
The first part of a story by one of Rod's ex-employees, Gail Williams, appears in *The Sun*.

8 May
Singer Linda Lewis is the latest to sell her story on Rod. The first part of her exposé appears in the *News Of The World*.

14 May
Rod plays in a charity football match at Wembley Stadium before the FA cup final.

16 May
'Lost In You' backed with 'Almost Illegal' is released as Rod's new single. Both are tracks from the forthcoming album 'Out Of Order'. It reaches No 21 in the UK and No 12 in the US.

20 May
Rod appears on BBC TV's *Terry Wogan Show*. He is interviewed and sings 'Lost In You'.

21 May
Rod achieves a life long ambition when he scores a goal at Wembley Stadium in a charity match before the Scotland-England game.

23 May
Rod releases a new studio album titled 'Out Of Order'. Produced by Rod, Andy Taylor and Bernard Edwards,

AT WEMBLEY STADIUM PLAYING IN THE MATCH WHERE HE SCORES A GOAL ON MAY 21, 1988.

it reaches No 11 in the UK and No 20 in the US.

Rod: "It's not just a return to roots. I'm still doing the same thing that I've always done - just better than I've done it for the last ten years or so. Returning to roots is really impossible. My use of words has become a bit more sophisticated, and whether that's a good thing or a bad thing I'm not sure. I'm confident that I'm a better songwriter now than I was in the days when I wrote 'Gasoline Alley'. There's more truth on this album than the last few and the song selection is better because we took the time to make it that way." (*Creem*)

30 May
Rod gives *Smiler* another exclusive interview and reveals

CELEBRATING WITH FATHER BOB STEWART AFTER SCORING A GOAL AT WEMBLEY ON MAY 21, 1988.

'SMILER' INTERVIEW, 30 MAY 1988.

that he is planning to include 'Mandolin Wind' and 'Every Picture Tells A Story' in his new live set.

ROD
"I think there's going to be a lot of taking the piss out of myself on this tour. That's what I want to do this time. Even in rehearsal I don't sing the songs in the same way, the new band also play them in a totally different way. We're going to do 'Every Picture Tells A Story' and maybe 'Mandolin Wind'. We've got to do some of the really old songs, there's a big upsurge in seventies music in America at the moment. If the demand is there, I'll play them."

31 May
In a *Daily Express* interview Rod says: "I don't want to be a sex symbol any more. I've

proved all that and it's so silly. I just want to be recognised for making good music and I don't even think I can make music for kids any more. I'm now making music for my own age group and maybe 15 years younger. I want to make mature rock'n'roll. I want to write and sing from experience and share it with people."

2 June

A scheduled live appearance by Rod on *Top Of The Pops* is called off because of an asbestos scare in TV studios. The studios are out of action whilst the asbestos is removed. It would have been Rod's first live appearance on the show for fifteen years.

4 June

Press reports suggest that Rod will marry Kelly Emberg this month.

15 June

Rod tells teen magazine *Smash Hits*: "I could definitely challenge The Beastie Boys to a hotel room smashing contest. I've been at it far too long for them. I've got the experience you see."

26 June

Rod talks to the *Sunday Express* magazine about his current standing in rock music: "You come to a point in your life where you say, 'What I've achieved is good enough.' I don't suppose I'll ever sell as many records as Michael Jackson or Bruce Springsteen so there's no point in kidding myself. But I'm very, very pleased with my own lot. I never dreamed it would last as long as this."

27 June

Rod appears again on the live

OUT OF ORDER, 1988.

phone-in radio show *Rockline* which is broadcast throughout most of the US.

JULY

Dates: San Juan, Puerto Rico *(1)*, Tampa Stadium, Tampa, Fla *(2)*, Joe Robbie Stadium, Fort Lauderdale, Fla *(3)*, Civic Center, Pensacola, Fla *(6)*, Coliseum Arena, Charlotte, NC *(8)*, Dean Smith Center, Chapel Hill, NC *(9)*, Scope Arena, Norfolk, Va *(10)*, Starwood Amphitheater, Nashville, Tenn *(12)*, Oak Mountain Amphitheater, Birmingham, Al *(13)*, The Arena, St Louis, Mo *(15)*, Barton Coliseum, Little Rock, Ark *(16)*, Hirsch Memorial Coliseum, Shreveport, La *(17)*, UNO Lakefront Arena, New Orleans, La *(20)*, The Summit, Houston, Tx *(21)*,

Starplex Amphitheater, Dallas, Tx *(23)*, Frank Erwin Center, Austin, Tx *(24)*, Lloyd Noble Center, Norman, Ok *(26)*, Sandstone Amphitheater, Kansas City, Mo *(27)*, Fiddler's Green Amphitheater, Denver, Co *(29)*, Salt Palace, Salt Lake City, Utah *(30)*.

1 July

Rod opens a five month American tour at the Hiram Bithorn Stadium, San Juan, Puerto Rico. Featuring a new band, it is the first solo tour Rod has made without guitarist Jim Cregan. Line up is Jeff Goulb (guitar), Stevie Salas (guitar), Carmine Rojas (bass), Tony Brock (drums), Chuck Kentis (keyboards), Rick Braun (trumpet/ keyboards), Nick Lane (trombone) and Jimmy

Roberts (saxophone).

The set for this tour features a selection of the following: 'Hot Legs', 'Infatuation', 'Tonight's The Night', 'Some Guys Have All The Luck', 'Young Turks', 'First Cut Is The Deepest', 'You're In My Heart', 'Sweet Little Rock'n'Roller', 'Lost In You', 'Dynamite', 'Forever Young', 'People Get Ready', 'I Ain't Superstitious', 'Mandolin Wind', 'Tear It Up', 'Da Ya Think I'm Sexy?', 'Passion', 'Stay With Me', 'Twistin' The Night Away'.

11 July

The 'Video Collection' release a video in the UK and Europe titled *Rod Stewart & The Faces': A Video Biography*. It contains an hour of live performances by The Faces.

AUGUST

Dates: The Coliseum, Seattle, Wash *(1)*, Lawlor Events Center, Reno, Na *(3)*, Mid State Fair, Paso Robles, Ca *(5)*, Devore Stadium, San Diego, Ca *(7)*, The Forum, Los Angeles, Ca *(9, 10 & 11)*, Shoreline Amphitheater, Mountain View, Ca *(14)*, Concord Pavilion, Concord, Ca *(16)*, PNE Pacific Coliseum, Vancouver, BC *(20)*, Saddledome, Calgary, Alberta *(22)*, CNE Stadium, Ottawa, Ontario *(27)*, Exhibition Stadium, Toronto, Ontario *(28)*, Performing Arts Center, Saratoga Springs, NY *(29)*, The Forum, Montreal, Quebec *(31)*.

1 August

Rod releases a new single, titled 'Forever Young', from the album 'Out Of Order'. The B-side, 'Days Of Rage', is exclusive to the single. It reaches No 57 in the UK and No 12 in the US.

23 August

Rod cancels a concert in Edmonton, Canada, due to a sore throat. He also cancels a concert in Winnipeg on the 25th. The dates are re-scheduled for November.

SEPTEMBER

Dates: Copps Coliseum, Hamilton, Ontario *(1)*, Jones Beach Theater, Wantaugh, NY *(17 & 18)*, Civic Center, Portland, Me *(19)*, The Centrum, Worcester, Mass *(22)*, Civic Center, Providence, RI *(23)*, The Garden, Boston, Mass (24), Madison Square Garden, New York *(26 & 27)*, The Spectrum, Philadelphia, Pa *(30)*.

In a rare interview in *Creem* magazine Rod says of his

MADISON SQUARE GARDEN, NEW YORK, SEPTEMBER 1988.

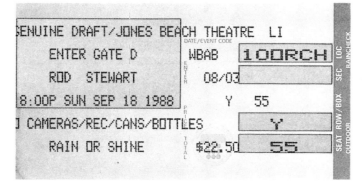

career: "I've worked harder and harder. The last two albums before this one ('Out Of Order') were a bit shaky, but I think I've stayed pretty true to the craft of songwriting and recording. I've gone off the rails a little bit since 'Da Ya Think I'm Sexy?' But I think I'm pretty well back on track now."

7 September
Rod appears at the MTV awards in New York.

The Sun reports that Rod has had a furious bust up with Sting. It started when Rod carved a rude message on the table of Sting's private plane which read: "Sting, you pompous bastard! When are you going to get a sense of humour?" Sting hit back by turning up with friends at Rod's Hollywood mansion and chaining up his electric gates while he was out. As workmen sawed them off, Rod spent the night in a hotel and was so furious, he called the police the next day. To show Rod he had a sense of humour, Sting sent him a bunch of flowers. The incident happened while they were both on a US tour. Sting had a few days off, so Rod borrowed his plane.

OCTOBER
Dates: The Coliseum, Richmond, Va *(1)*, Thompson-Boling Arena, Knoxville, Tenn *(2)*, The Palace, Detroit, Mi *(18 & 19)*, Rupp Arena, Lexington Centre, Lexington, Ky *(20)*, The Omni, Atlanta, Ga *(30)*.

30 October
The *Sunday People* reports that Rod has been told by his doctor to quit singing and give his throat a long rest, otherwise he risks losing his voice for good. This follows the cancellation of a show at Bloomington, Minnesota.

NOVEMBER
Dates: Pacific Amphitheater, Costa Mesa, Ca *(11)*, Coliseum, Phoenix, Az *(12)*, Arco Arena, Sacremento, Ca *(14)*, Northlands Coliseum, Edmonton, Alberta *(18)*, Winnipeg Arena, Winnipeg,

LIVE ON THE 'OUT OF ORDER' TOUR, 1988.

Manitoba *(21 & 22)*, Maple Leaf Gardens, Toronto, Ontario *(24)*, The Forum, Montreal, Quebec *(25)*, Hartford Civic Center, Hartford, Ct *(29)*, Meadowlands Arena, NJ *(30)*.

13 November
The *Sunday People* reports that a top American radio station has banned all Rod's records until he makes up for all the cancelled shows on his tour.

13 November
According to the *News Of The World*, Rod is about to take his wife, Alana, to court so he can marry Kelly Emberg. Alana will not give him a

divorce until she gets more money. A friend says: "He and Alana made a pre-marriage agreement and she's already had more than that. He's bought her a £2 million house in California and he pays for her secretary, a cook and a full time nanny for their two children."

25 November
The Sun reports that songs from Rod's album 'Foolish Behaviour' have been used by US spy chiefs to send coded messages to agents behind the Iron Curtain. The operation was codenamed 'Hot Legs'! Rod is said to be furious and intends to sue the CIA.

DECEMBER
Dates: Civic Arena, Pittsburgh, Pa *(2)*, The Coliseum, Richfield, Ohio *(3)*, Market Square Arena, Indianapolis, Ind *(4)*, Charleston Civic Center, Charleston, Va *(10)*, Capitol Center, Landover, Mi *(11)*.

Rod's 'Out Of Order' album is named as the eleventh best selling album of the year in Canada. In America the album is awarded two platinum discs for sales in excess of two million, while in Britain it earns a gold disc for sales of more than 100,000.

A new single is released in the US titled 'My Heart Can't Tell You No'. It goes on to reach No 4 in the chart, making it Rod's biggest hit of the decade.

10 December
Rod's manager, Arnold Stiefel, lands a development deal with Columbia Pictures for a film called *Maggie May*, a film about a teenage boy/older woman romance based on Rod's hit of the same name.

1989

2 January
The Sun reports that Rod and six of his mates dropped their trousers whilst having a meal at Brooklyn's trendy River Café in New York. Not to be outdone, a female friend who was with the party got her boobs out!

January
Rod is nominated for a Grammy, America's top rock and pop award.

10 January
Rod celebrates his 44th birthday at London's Langan's Brasserie with Kelly Emberg and Ron Wood.

24 January
Commenting to waiting reporters at Heathrow Airport, Rod says: "My album ('Out Of Order') did really well in the

WITH SINGER SHEENA EASTON AT THE AMERICAN MUSIC AWARDS, JANUARY 30, 1989.

WITH KELLY EMBERG, EARLY 1989.

States. But I was disappointed that it didn't do so well over here."

29 January
The *Sunday People* reports that Rod is looking for a teenage lookalike to star in a £10 million movie being produced by Columbia pictures based on his years in rock'n'roll. Arnold Stiefel comments: "Rod will be providing the musical soundtrack only. There is absolutely no way he is prepared to act."

30 January
Rod co-hosts the 16th annual American Music Awards show at the Shrine Auditorium, Los Angeles. He also performs 'My Heart Can't Tell You No' and 'Forever Young'.

15 February
Rod joins the ranks of celebrities signed up by Pepsi Cola to advertise the soft drink. The adverts are only used in South America.

MARCH
Date: Club Olympia, Sao Paulo, Brazil *(29)*.

APRIL
Dates: Palmeiros Football Stadium, Rio de Janeiro, Brazil *(2)*, Queretaro, Mexico *(9)*, Costa Mesa Pacific Amphitheater, Ca *(14 & 15)*, Starplex Amphitheater, Dallas, Tx *(21)*, Cajundome, Lafayette, La *(22)*, The Summit, Houston, Tx *(23)*, Lakefront Arena, New Orleans, La *(26)*, Sun Dome, Tampa, Fla *(27)*, Orlando Arena, Orlando, Fla *(28)*.

'My Heart Can't Tell You No' backed with 'The Wild Horse' is released in the UK and reaches No 49 on the charts.

4 April
Channel Four screen an hour long documentary about Rod titled *The Story Of Rod Stewart*.

MAY
Dates: Coliseum, Charlotte, NC *(7)*, RPI Fieldhouse, Troy, NY *(9)*, Civic Center, Ottawa, Ontario *(10)*, The Forum, Montreal, Quebec *(12)*, Moncton Coliseum, Moncton, New Brunswick (16), Metro Center, Halifax, NS, *(23, 24 & 25)*, Great Woods, Boston, Mass *(28 & 29)*, Mann Music Center, Philadelphia, Pa *(31)*.

A fourth single from 'Out Of Order' is released in the US: 'Crazy About Her' backed with 'Dynamite'. It is also available in several different mixes. It reaches No 11 in the US but is never released in Britain.

BACKSTAGE AT MADISON SQUARE GARDEN WITH ELDER BROTHER DON STEWART AND HIS WIFE PAT.

2 May
Rod announces that his only live European appearance of 1989 will be at a charity show in Paris on June 24.

19 May
Rod flies into Britain with Kelly Emberg to watch the FA Cup Final.

JUNE
Dates: Mann Music Center, Philadelphia, Pa *(1)*, Nassau Coliseum, Uniondale, NY *(2)*, Sydney Center, Sydney, Nova Scotia *(5)*, Moncton Coliseum, Moncton, New Brunswick *(6)*, Skydome, Toronto, On *(8)*, Hersheypark Stadium, Hershey, Pa *(9)*, M.P. Pavilion, Columbia, Md *(10)*, Garden State Art Center, Holmdel, NJ *(14)*, Memorial Auditorium, Buffalo, NY *(16)*, Blossom Music Center, Cuyahuga Falls, Ohio *(17)*, Deer Creek Amphitheater, Indianapolis, Ind *(18)*, The Muni, St. Louis, Mo *(27)*, Mid-South Coliseum,

Memphis, Tenn *(28)*, Coliseum, Jackson, Miss *(30)*.

1 June
Rod's ex-wife, Alana, asks a court to increase her maintenance payments to nearly £50,000 a month, a rise of 300%!

4 June
The *News Of The World* reports that Rod has been invited by Russian leader Mikhail Gorbachev to perform a concert in Moscow. He is also invited to dine with the leader and his wife.

23 June
Jesse Ed Davis, who played with The Faces on their final tour and appeared on Rod's 'Atlantic Crossing' album, dies aged 43 in California, apparently from a heroin overdose.

24 June
A massive charity concert starring Rod Stewart, George

Michael and Stevie Wonder is scrapped. The Liberty show was to be held in Paris and would have raised £1,000,000 for UNICEF, but French police objected to it because they felt they would not be able to control the 75,000 crowd.

JULY
Dates: Pine Knob Amphitheater, Detroit, Mi *(5 & 6)*, Summerfest, Milwaukee, Wis *(7)*, Smith Center, Chapel Hill, NC *(9)*, Winnipeg Arena, Winnipeg, Manitoba *(10)*, Saskatchewan Palace, Saskatoon, SK *(11)*, The Saddledome, Calgary, Alberta *(12)*, Amphitheater, George, Wash, *(15)*, B.C. Place Stadium, Vancouver, BC *(16)*, Cal Expo Amphitheater, Sacramento, Ca *(22)*, Concord Pavilion, Concord, Ca *(23)*, Hollywood Bowl, Los Angeles, Ca *(31)*.

5 July
On the first night at Pine

Knob Amphitheater, about 90 minutes into the set, Rod runs towards the back of the stage to an elevated area behind the drummer, cuts a corner too closely and slams the front of his head into a lighting fixture. He collapses and falls, face forward, to the floor. The spotlight is taken off him, and gradually the band realise something is wrong and stop playing. A couple of fans mop Rod's head with a towel and after about a minute, crew members walk Rod off stage. Twenty minutes later he returns, unbandaged, but in a different shirt and vest. After apologising to the crowd he launches into 'Hot Legs'.

29 July
In an article published in the *Los Angeles Times*, Paul Grein talks to Rod's manager Arnold Stiefel, rock-orientated radio programmer, Stephanie Mondello and Rod about his past image problems.

Grein writes: "Rod Stewart and his managers mapped out a plan six years ago in an effort to restore the performer's sagging rock'n'roll credibility. The plan has succeeded beyond their expectations. The forthcoming Bowl concert is Stewart's seventh Los Angeles concert in less than a year.

His current tour, originally scheduled to run for four months, is now in its 13th. His current album 'Out Of Order' has sold nearly two million copies in the United States since its release in mid-1988 and has yielded four straight top 15 singles. Many, including Stewart and his managers, credit his comeback to his success at downplaying his old persona as a jet-setting playboy. The image, which began to develop in the mid 70s, was cemented in 1979 by the glitzy disco hit 'Da Ya Think I'm Sexy?'

Grein: "That's why Stewart and his advisers decided to release the rocker 'Lost In You' as the first single from 'Out of Order' rather than the more obvious ballads 'Forever Young' and 'My Heart Can't Tell You No'."

Stephanie Mondello (Music director at album-rock mainstay KLOS-FM): "He's definitely back in the album-rock mainstream. If you put a rock record out you'll be played on rock radio. If you don't you won't. And with this album, he's back to his rock'n'roll roots. He did do the pop/dance stuff, but prior to that he was one of the cornerstones of album-rock radio, one of the superstars who started the format."

Stiefel's partner, Randy Phillips: "It was a struggle to get rock radio stations to play 'Lost In You'. It was like a dogfight. We faced

tremendous resistance because it was Rod. But I think people are rediscovering what they liked about him in the old days - things that were obscured with some of the disco and more Top 40 stuff he did."

AUGUST
Dates: Sports Arena, San Diego, Ca *(1)*, Wang Center, Boston, Mass *(5)*, Seashore PAC, Old Orchard Beach, Me *(8)*, Lake Compounce Festival Park, Bristol, Ct *(10)*, Meadowlands Arena, East Rutherford, NJ *(11)*, Quidi Vidi Park, St John's, Newfoundland *(13)*.

5 August
This Boston concert is a benefit for the American Cancer Society in honour of Canadian Terry Fox who died aged 22 on September 1, 1981. Fox, who was fitted with an artificial limb at 18, tried to run across Canada to raise awareness of cancer. He ran 3,339 miles from St John's, Newfoundland, to Northern Ontario in 144 days. His journey ended when the pain from his spreading cancer became unbearable.

Terry's mother, Betty, flew from Vancouver to attend the concert and afterwards presented Rod with an honorary award expressing her appreciation for his support.

5 September
Rod, Kelly Emberg and Ruby fly from Heathrow to Malaga in Spain for a family holiday.

17 September
Rod, Kelly Emberg and Ruby fly into Heathrow from Spain to change planes as they head back to their Los Angeles home.

OCTOBER
A new single is released in the US titled 'Downtown Train' from the 'Storyteller' album.

HOUNDED BY AUTOGRAPH HUNTERS ON THE US TOUR, 1989.

In 1990, it goes on to reach No 3 on the *Billboard* Chart, although it reaches No 1 on the *Cashbox* charts.

23 October
A new single is released in Britain, a new version of 'This Old Heart Of Mine' backed with 'Ain't Love A Bitch'. Ronald Isley is also featured on the record. It is taken from the forthcoming 'Best Of' album and reaches No 51.

24 October
Crippled Rod Stewart fan Colin Jones is awarded £625,000 damages for being injured at a concert in Earls Court in 1983. The agreed damages and costs are against Harvey Goldsmith Entertainments, Kennedy Street Enterprises, Earls Court Ltd, Tubular Barriers Ltd and the London Residuary Body.

6 November
A compilation album of Rod's best known hits is released in

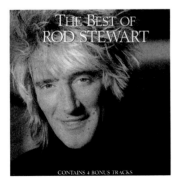

Britain and it crashes into the UK chart at its peak position of No 3. It is not released in the US where the CD only set 'Storyteller' is released, which reaches No 54.

16 November
Rod tells Radio One DJ Simon Bates that he has scrapped a European tour planned for 1990 in order to watch Scotland play in the World Cup Finals.

24 November
Rod refuses to appear at a 'Grammy Living Legends' show. He reportedly didn't want to be grouped with the other nominees, including Andrew Lloyd Webber and Liza Minelli, because it would be bad for his image. He had agreed to be on the show when he thought the other honorees might include Bob Dylan and Michael Jackson but pulled

ROD
"This whole project became a way to clean the slate, to make way for the Nineties. It's also an accurate portrayal of where I am today. No regrets, no apologies: take me for what I am because I'm certainly not going to remake myself."

WITH CRIPPLED FAN COLIN JONES.

out when the rest of the field was announced.

4 December
'Storyteller', a lavishly packaged set of 64 songs that trace Rod's career from 1964's 'Good Morning Little Schoolgirl' to 1989's 'Downtown Train', is released in a limited edition in the UK.

9 December
The *Daily Star* reports that Rod has revealed he needed singing lessons to save his career. He booked classes with

top coach Nate Lamb before recording 'Downtown Train'.

31 December
Rod visits crippled fan Colin Jones at his East End home. Colin was injured in a tragic accident at one of Rod's concerts at Earls Court in 1983. Rod went to see him laden with gifts, including a signed copy of the boxed set 'Storyteller', and the original gold disc from his first hit 'Maggie May'. Colin's mum Pat said: "Rod has made the day for Colin."

1990

1 January
'Downtown Train', backed with 1976's 'The Killing Of Georgie', is released as Rod's new single in the Britain. It reaches No 10 on the UK charts.

15 January
Rod appears on the live American phone-in radio show *Rockline*.

19 January
Rod is sued by fan Charles Falterman for being too sexy on stage! He is accused of being too erotic and provocative during his US tour. Lawyers claim Rod "whipped the fans into a boiling pot of sexual ecstasy leading to gross abandon". Due to the excited fans, Falterman was knocked down and suffered a broken knee. A friend of Rod says they will fight the case.

27 January
Rod appears on the *Michael Aspel Show*. He performs 'Downtown Train' and gives an interview in which he says he is close to marrying his long time girlfriend Kelly Emberg.

FEBRUARY
Rod performs 'Downtown Train' at the annual Brit Awards at London's Dominion Theatre.

MARCH
'This Old Heart Of Mine' is released in the US and reaches No 10 on the charts.

A compilation album featuring tracks from the boxed set 'Storyteller' is released in the US. It reaches No 20 on the charts.

PERFORMING 'DOWNTOWN TRAIN' AT THE BRIT AWARDS, FEBRUARY 1990.

4 March
Rod gives the UK fan club magazine *Smiler* an exclusive interview and reveals plans for a European tour early in 1991.

ROD
"There will be three or four football grounds along with indoor gigs. We'll be doing Old Trafford and all the others in between. When I looked at the tour we were going to do early this year, we had ten nights booked at Wembley Arena, three nights booked at Glasgow, five at the NEC in Birmingham and some at Milton Keynes Bowl. It was all booked for August, September and October."

9 March
Rod and his football team, the LA Exiles, play a match against the Portland Timbers at the Portland Civic Center in Oregon. The game is a benefit

MARCH 4, 1990

to raise money for the Oregon Chapter of the Multiple Sclerosis Society.

18 March
Rod appears at the Canadian Juno Awards at the O'Keefe Center, Toronto.

25 July
The *Daily Mirror* reports that Rod's girlfriend Kelly Emberg is moving out of the Los Angeles home they share to a beach house. She will also

take the couple's daughter, Ruby. Friends say their seven year romance is over.

27 July
The press reports that Rod is dating Helen Fairbrother, a 23-year old model from Solihull, Birmingham, England. She has been spotted with Rod at several London restaurants and night clubs.

1 August
The Sun reports that Rod and Tina Turner have recorded a duet of the Tamla Motown hit 'It Takes Two' for a new £2,000,000 television advertising campaign for Diet Pepsi. Rod recorded his part in a studio in Los Angeles and Tina recorded her part in London as both singers were too busy to meet up at the same studio.

14 September
Rod and his family attend the funeral of his father Bob Stewart who died aged 85. At a quiet family ceremony at St Michaels Church in Highgate, North London, Rod and his brothers Don and Bob arrange floral displays like a football pitch with players and balls and a Scottish flag as a tribute to their soccer mad father.

17 October
The new single by Rod and Tina Turner, 'It Takes Two', is named by bookies as second favourite to be No 1 at Christmas at 8-1. Reports say that Rod and Tina are set to pocket between one to five million pounds from a new Diet Pepsi Cola commercial. The video for the single was filmed in France.

24 October
Rod announces that he is to marry 21-year old Rachel Hunter just two months after they met.

10 November
A woman sues Rod, claiming she was hurt at one of his concerts. Patricia Boughton of Utica, New York State, claims she suffered a ruptured tendon in her middle finger and a possible break when she was struck by a soccer ball kicked out by Rod during a performance at the Pine Knob Music Theater on June 22, 1989. The lawsuit seeks at least $10,000 in damages.

12 November
'It Takes Two' backed with 'Hot Legs' from 'Absolutely Live' is released as the new single by Rod and Tina Turner. It reaches No 5 on the UK charts.

30 November
Tina Turner pulls out of a joint concert with Rod at the last minute because she is tired of touring. The concert was to have taken place in Germany during December and shown on televison around the world.

15 December
Rod marries 21-year-old Rachel Hunter at the Beverley Hills Presbyterian Church, California. The ceremony is

ROD TIES THE KNOT AT THE BEVERLEY HILLS PRESBYTERIAN CHURCH ON DECEMBER 15, 1990.

very much a family affair, with relatives of the couple far outnumbering the celebrities. After the ceremony a London style double decker bus carries most of the guests the two miles to the exclusive Four Seasons Hotel for the reception. Guests are seated at tables decorated with the names of British football teams, among them West Ham, Bolton Wanderers and Liverpool. The meal is a traditional British feast of roast lamb with mint sauce, roast potatoes and sprouts. The three foot tall wedding cake is a replica of the Houses of Parliament and Big Ben, with a giant kiwi on the roof in honour of Rachel's New Zealand connections.

17 December
Rod and his bride fly to Britain for their honeymoon.

Good Morning, Are You Sitting Down?
Rachel Hunter
and
Rod Stewart
request the honour of your presence
at their marriage
on Saturday, the fifteenth of December
Nineteen hundred and ninety
at four o'clock
Beverly Hills Presbyterian Church
Rodeo Drive at Santa Monica Boulevard
Beverly Hills, California

1991

1 January
Rod celebrates the New Year at a party in London at The Ritz Hotel.

18 February
USA Today reports that Rod's ex-girlfriend Kelly Emberg is to sue him for $25 million. They reveal that on December 18 Emberg filed court papers in Los Angeles claiming Rod failed to pay her the $20,000 a month she claims he verbally promised, and that she is now seeking part of his fortune on top of these payments.

KELLY EMBERG
"Although Rod has promised me that he would always take care of our daughter and me, suddenly he is trying to deny us the life we have come to know. He has not given me any money except for $3,000 for the four months of our separation and the use of some of his credit cards for expenses for Ruby's clothing, toys and some food."

ROD
"I'm not about to get bogged down in all those subpoenas, depositions and court appearances. I know what Kelly is up to with this, and it simply won't work. She won't get a bloody penny off me for herself. I don't mind supporting Ruby, but I'll be damned if I'm going to pay for Kelly to live in the grand style that she lived in while she was with me. Why should she live like I do?"

20 February
Rod and his wife Rachel attend the 33rd annual Grammy awards at Radio City Music Hall, New York. Rod is nominated for best 'Male Pop Vocal' for his single 'Downtown Train' but does not win.

MARCH
Dates: Exhibiton Centre, Aberdeen *(25 & 26)*, King's Hall, Belfast *(30)*.

4 March
'Rhythm Of My Heart' backed with 'Moment Of Glory' is released as Rod's new single. It reaches No 3 on the UK charts and No 5 on the US charts. Both are tracks from the forthcoming album 'Vagabond Heart'.

9 March
Rod appears on London Weekend Television's *Michael Aspel Show*. He gives an interview and performs his single 'Rhythm Of My Heart'.

11 March
Rod gives *Q* magazine an interview at Elstree Studios during rehearsals for his forthcoming tour.

22 March
Status Quo are announced as support act on Rod's forthcoming stadium shows.

25 March
Rod releases his new album 'Vagabond Heart'. It reaches No 2 on the UK charts and No 10 on the US charts.

ROD
"I looked at the charts yesterday and there were only me and Queen and Free there from the old days. And Free are only there because of the Levi's ad. And not even Queen were around in 1971. Yeah, I've definitely seen them all come and go. The reviews do worry me. But then I don't think Van Morrison is the happiest person on this earth and I am, and that's what counts. Reviews can never give you that. And the fans have stayed loyal. I get letters! People say, I've been a fan of yours for 15 years... can you lend us a fiver 'till the weather breaks?

"I wasn't very keen on that Madonna show. I'd rather sit in a dentist's chair for half an hour. I don't even know if she's singing but the band aren't playing and it takes the arse out of rock'n'roll. Too camp, too gay. There's always got to be an element of mistakes in rock'n'roll, an element of risk. It's got to fall down sometimes, a bit of out of tune singing, otherwise it's sterile and void of any soul." *(Q Magazine)*

25 & 26 March
Rod starts his first European tour in over four years at Aberdeen. The band for this tour consists of Carmine Rojas (bass), Jeff Goulb (guitar), Todd Sharp (guitar), Dave Palmer (drums), Nick Lane (trombone), Rick Braun (trumpet/keyboards), Jimmy Roberts (saxophone), Darryl Phinnesse and Dorian Holly (backing vocals).

The set changes throughout the tour and is made up of a selection of the following: 'Tonight I'm Yours', 'Sweet Little Rock'n' Roller', 'This Old Heart Of Mine', 'Downtown Train', 'Hot Legs', 'Tonight's The Night', 'First Cut Is The Deepest', 'Passion', 'Go Out Dancing', 'Every Beat Of My Heart', 'Sweet Soul Music', 'Sittin' On The Dock Of The Bay', 'Time Is Tight', 'Every Picture Tells A Story', 'Mandolin Wind', 'You're In My Heart', 'Muddy Waters

Blues', 'Baby Jane', 'Some Guys Have All The Luck', 'Reason To Believe', 'Maggie May', 'You Wear It Well', 'I Don't Want To Talk About It', 'Sailing', 'Twistin' The Night Away', 'It Takes Two', 'Stay With Me', 'The Motown Song'.

APRIL
Dates: Wembley Arena, London *(1, 2, 4 & 5)*, NEC, Birmingham *(9, 10 & 11)*, Maastricht, Holland *(14)*, Antwerp, Belgium *(16)*, The Globe, Stockholm, Sweden *(19 & 20)*, Kiel, Germany *(24)*, Westfalenhalle, Dortmund, Germany *(28)*.

Rod is ordered to pay $13,000 a month in child support to Kelly Emberg for their daughter Ruby.

1 April
During the first night at Wembley, Elton John joins

Rod on stage wearing a black and gold frilly dress, stockings, high heels and a blonde wig. Whilst Rod sings 'You're In My Heart', Elton sits on his knee and serves him brandy from a silver tray. The prank was set up as an April Fool's joke by Rod's management.

14 April
Rod is furious when the *News Of The World* prints pictures of him and Rachel sun bathing in the back garden of his Epping mansion. Rod says the photos are an invasion of his privacy and therefore break the newspapers' code of conduct.

The photos are said to have been taken from a public footpath by a freelance photographer.

17 April
Rod cancels a concert in Gothenburg, Sweden, due to a sore throat. A second concert in Stockholm on April 21 is also cancelled.

21 April
The *News Of The World* publicly apologises to Rod for printing the pictures of him and Rachel sun bathing which appeared in the previous week's issue.

26 April
Rod cancels a show in Cologne, Germany, again due to throat problems.

MAY
Dates: Pattnoire De Malley, Lausanne, Switzerland *(2)*, Olympiahalle, Munich, Germany *(4 & 5)*,

ELTON PROVES TO BE A REAL DRAG AT ROD'S APRIL 1 WEMBLEY ARENA CONCERT.

Eissporthalle, Kassel, Germany *(8)*, Eisstadion, Memmingen, Germany *(9)*, Arena, Verona, Italy *(12)*, Patinoire de Malley, Lausanne, Switzerland *(12)*, Hallenstadion, Zurich, Switzerland *(14 & 15)*, Stadthalle, Vienna, Austria *(17)*, Festhalle, Frankfurt, Germany *(19)*, Schleyerhalle, Frankfurt, Germany *(24 & 25)*, Albgaustadion, Karlsruhe, Germany *(26)*, Waldbuehne, Berlin, Germany *(29)*.

12 May
Two songs from this concert, 'Sweet Soul Music' and 'Rhythm Of My Heart', are beamed live to Wembley Arena and broadcast live on BBC2 as part of the 'Simple Truth' concert in aid of Kurdish refugees.

22 May
Rod cancels a concert in Lyon, France, at the last minute after suffering a throat infection.

31 May
The Sun reports that Rod could possibly cancel the remainder of his world tour after having to pull out of his fourth show in three weeks with throat problems.

JUNE
Dates: Celtic Park, Glasgow *(1)*, Gateshead, Newcastle *(2)*, The Arena, Sheffield *(4)*, Old Trafford, Manchester *(7)*, Gateshead, Newcastle *(9)*, Portman Road, Ipswich *(12 & 13)*, Wembley Stadium, London *(15)*, SEC, Glasgow *(17)*, Sporthalle, Cologne, Germany *(18)*, Volksparkstadion, Hamburg, Germany *(21)*, Stadion, Bayreuth, Germany *(22)*, Palais Omnisport, Paris *(24 & 25)*, Ahoy, Rotterdam,

Holland *(27)*, RDS, Dublin *(29)*, Festival, Hanover, Germany *(30)*.

1 June
Rod starts a series of football stadium dates around Britain at Celtic Park. He is supported by Status Quo and Joe Cocker.

3 June
Rod postpones a second concert at Gateshead Stadium in Newcastle due to throat problems. The date is rearranged for June 9.

5 June
The local press in Sheffield report that Rod's show in the city was a total 'wash out' lasting only eighty minutes. They say he had no energy, a very poor voice and omitted many big hits, including 'Baby Jane'. Many fans demanded their money back. Later it was revealed that the medication Rod had been taking to overcome his throat problems had made him drowsy.

ROD
"I had to take fucking cortisone, which is like a steroid and what it did was made my throat swell up. That was the trouble in Sheffield and a lot of people didn't know what was going on. I was supposed to take the pills on a full stomach with a glass of milk, but I'd been taking them on an empty stomach! I was bleeding internally for an hour and a half while I was on stage. I shouldn't have gone on. It was one time I should have said to everybody 'Go home'." *(Smiler)*

6 June
Rod postpones another concert at the Scottish Exhibition Centre in Glasgow. The show is rearranged for June 17.

12 & 13 June
Council health officers force organisers to turn down the

volume at the second Ipswich concert due to a barrage of complaints about noise from the first. Controversy erupted after headteachers said children's exams were disrupted, court proceedings were halted and large numbers of local residents complained. Daytime soundchecks are also banned, as they had caused the complaints from schools.

BACKSTAGE IN PARIS ON JUNE 25, 1991, WITH OFFICIAL FAN CLUB SECRETARY STEVE HOLMES.

28 June
Elton John presents Rod with the Nordoff Robbins Silver Clef award at a ceremony in London. Rod also makes an impromptu award to Elton when he gets his wife, Rachel, to hand him a music box with the inscription: 'To my dear Sharon, my left leg has never been the same - love Philis.'

It is a reference to the April Fool's joke Elton played on Rod earlier in the year.

Rod commented: "I've bought Elton a music box and I paid a lot for the fucking thing. I thought, it's a long time since Elton got his hand on a big box."

29 June
Rod is joined on stage by Chris De Burgh at this concert and the pair duet on 'Sailing'.

JULY
Dates: Milan, Italy *(10)*,

Manker, Mannheim, Germany *(12)*, Loreley Freilichtbuhne, Germany *(13)*, Vienna, Austria *(16)*, Hamburg, Germany *(20)*, NEC, Birmingham *(23)*, G-Mex, Manchester *(26)*, Fitzgerald Stadium, Killarney *(27)*.

Rod gives his first interview to *Rolling Stone* magazine for ten years and appears on the front cover with his wife Rachel. He comments: "I should say it's about time they put a bit of class on the cover again. It's usually scumbags on the cover. I've never heard of who's on the cover sometimes."

20 July
The Hamburg show is televised live across Europe by Sky television. It attracts an estimated audience of 100 million.

23 July
Following several cancelled and postponed concerts on the European tour, Rod tells *Today* newspaper: "I have had a terrible time worrying about the voice. I don't want to talk about this for these thoughts are so awful. My voice is my life. It has taken a terrible pounding. I have a virus infection which has affected the vocal cords. The awful spring weather caused setbacks. For example, there was hail and sleet during my Wembley show. I have already sung in front of more than a million fans this summer. I don't want to disappoint them."

AUGUST
Dates: Halifax, Nova Scotia *(17)*, Performing Arts Center, Saratoga, NY *(20)*, Seashore Performing Arts Center, Portland, Me *(21 - this concert was originally scheduled for August 19, but cancelled due to Hurricane Bob)*, The Centrum, Worcester, Me *(23 & 24)*, Starlake Amphitheater, Burgettstown, Pa *(26)*, Blossom Music Center, Cuyahoga Falls, Ohio *(27)*, CNE Grandstand, Toronto, Ontario *(29)*, Lansdowne Park, Ottawa, Ontario *(30)*.

5 August
Headline publish a new biography of Rod written by Tim Ewbank and Stafford Hildred. Imaginatively titled *Rod Stewart - A Biography*, it was published both in hardback and paperback..

17 August
Rod starts the North American leg of the 'Vagabond Heart' tour at the 40,000 capacity Citidel Hill, Halifax, Nova Scotia in Canada.

Several new songs are added to the set for this leg of the tour, including: 'Infatuation', 'Lost In You', 'Forever Young', 'My Heart Can't Tell You No', 'Broken Arrow', 'In The Midnight Hour' and 'Young Turks'.

26 August
'Broken Arrow' backed with 1984's 'Some Guys Have All The Luck' is released as Rod's new single. It makes No 54 on the UK charts and 20 on the US charts.

SEPTEMBER
Dates: Nutter Center, Dayton, Ohio *(2)*, Marcus Amphitheater, Milwaukee, Wi *(5)*, Fiddler's Green, Denver, Co *(7)*, Concord Pavilion, Concord, Ca *(10)*, Shoreline, San Jose, Ca *(11)*, Pacific Amphitheater, Costa Mesa, Ca *(13, 14 & 15)*, Poplar Creek Music Theater, Chicago, Ill *(19 & 20)*, Deer Creek Music Theater, Indianopolis, Ind *(21)*, Meadowlands, East Rutherford, NJ *(24, 26 & 27)*, Carrier Dome, Syracuse, NY *(28)*.

1 September
Merriweather Post Pavilion, Columbia, Md.

22 September
The *Sunday People* reports that Rod has scrapped the promotional video for his new single 'Broken Arrow'. In the £250,000 video Rod is seen singing on rooftops late at night in a long mac and trilby while his wife, Rachel, poses on a cliff top. The reason given for Rod scrapping the video is that he was unhappy with the way he looked.

OCTOBER
Dates: The Spectrum, Philadelphia, Pa *(1 & 2)*, Blockbuster Pavilion, Charlotte, NC *(4)*, Walnut Creek Amphitheater, Raleigh, NC *(5)*, Starwood Amphitheater, Nashville, Tenn *(6)*, Suncoast Dome, St. Petersburg, Fla *(12)*, Miami Arena, Miami, Fla *(13 & 14)*, Lakewood Amphitheater, Atlanta, Ga *(17)*, Superdome, New Orleans, La *(18)*, Tallahassee, Fla *(19)*, Cynthia Woods Mitchell Pavilion, Houston, Tx *(22 & 23)*, Starplex Amphitheater, Dallas, Tx *(25)*, Kansas City, Mo *(26)*, Target Center Arena, Minneapolis, Minn *(27)*, Memphis, Tenn *(30)*.

14 October
The Canadian rock band Glass Tiger release a single titled 'My Town' on which Rod appears singing a duet with lead singer Alan Frew and also on backing vocals. The song is a track from the album 'Simple Mission' produced by Jim Cregan. It reaches No 34 on the UK charts.

Also released is an album entitled 'Two Rooms' which features various artists performing cover versions of

Elton John/Bernie Taupin compositions. Rod's contribution is 'Your Song'.

NOVEMBER

Dates: Thompson Boling Assembly Center & Arena, Knoxville, Tenn *(1)*, Jefferson Arena, Birmingham, Al *(2)*, Louisville, Ky *(6)*, Civic Center, Providence, RI *(9)*, Nassau Coliseum, Nassau, NY *(12 & 13)*, The Forum, Montreal, Quebec *(19)*, The Spectrum, Philadelphia, Pa *(21)*, The Palace, Detroit, Mi *(23 & 24)*.

24 November
Rod trips over a microphone cable in Detroit and injures his ankle, causing a hairline fracture. A concert planned for November 25 is immediately cancelled.

25 November
Warners release a new home video titled 'Rod Stewart - The Videos 1984 - 1991.' It features a collection of promotional videos.

DECEMBER

Dates: Northlands Coliseum, Edmonton, Alberta *(4)*, The Saddledome, Calgary, Alberta *(6 & 7)*, BC Palace, Vancouver, British Columbia *(9)*, Tacoma Dome, Tacoma, Washington *(10)*, Sports Arena, San Diego, Ca *(13)*, Blockbuster Desert Sky Pavilion, Phoenix, Az *(14)*, Sports Palace, Mexico City *(18, 19 & 20)*.

22 December
Rod flies into Britain with his wife Rachel to spend Christmas with his family.

ROD BEING INTERVIEWED BY 'SMILER' ON JANUARY 2, 1992

POSTSCRIPT

With this extraordinary workload behind him Rod Stewart might be expected to take things easy but as we said at the beginning he's still a grafter and it's unlikely he'll be adopting the traditional megastar routine of regular impermanent 'retirements' yet.

As this book went to press Rod's 'Vagabond Heart' tour was in its thirteenth month. Following the Christmas break in England, the tour resumed on January 11 at the Freedom Hall in Louisville, Kentucky, and was scheduled to run through the following North American cities through the winter: Greensboro *(January 12)*, Charleston *(14)*, Richfield *(15)*, Rosemount *(17)*, Landover *(19)*, Pittsburgh *(20)*, Toronto *(22)*, Worcester *(23)*, Hartford *(24)*, New York *(27 &28)*, Boston *(29)*, Detroit *(February 1& 2)*, Memphis *(4)*, Los Angeles *(7, 9 & 10)*, Oakland *(12)* and Universal City *(14)*. In March the tour is scheduled to head for Australia with dates in Brisbane *(3)*, Sydney *(6 & 7)*, Adelaide *(11)*, Melbourne *(17 & 18)* and Perth *(22)*. If things go as planned, the tour will grind to a halt in New Zealand in mid-April but knowing Rod's enthusiasm for his art, it could easily be extended.

On January 2, 1992, Rod spoke at length with the editor of *Smiler* and said he would be starting a new studio album during the summer which he hoped would be released in late 1992 or the spring of 1993. He also promised another European tour within two years. On a personal note, he said he'd never been happier. His wife Rachel is expecting her first baby in June and it really does now seem as if Rod has found the right person with whom to spend the rest of his life.

Whatever path Rod takes in the future, one thing is certain: he will continue to entertain the tabloids with his escapades and the fans with his music. He still claims not to have produced the masterpiece of an album that he really wants to create, so - in the words of his boyhood idol Al Jolson - you ain't seen nothing yet!

SINGLES

You'll Be Mine/Up Above My Head
United Artists *1056, 1964 (With John Baldry - uncredited duet on B-side)*

Good Morning Little Schoolgirl/I'm Gonna Move To The Outskirts Of Town
Decca *F 11996, 1964*

The Day Will Come/Why Does It Go On
Columbia *DB 7766, 1965*

Shake/I Just Got Some
Columbia *DB 7892, 1966*

I Could Feel The Whole World Turn Round Underneath Me/Curtains (instrumental) Columbia *DB 8025, 1966 (With Shotgun Express)*

Tallyman (instrumental)/Rock My Plimsoul Columbia *DB 8227, 1967 (with Jeff Beck - Rod featured on B-side only)*

Love Is Blue (instrumental)/I've Been Drinking Columbia *DB 8359, 1968 (with Jeff Beck - Rod featured on B-side only)*

Little Missunderstood/So Much To Say
Immediate *IM 060, 1968*

In A Broken Dream/Doing Fine
Youngblood *YB 1017, 1970 (with Python Lee Jackson)*

It's All Over Now/Jo's Lament
Vertigo *6086 002, 1970*

Flying/Three Button Hand Me Down
Warner Bros *WB 8005, 1970) (with The Faces)*

Had Me A Real Good Time/Rear Wheel Skid (instrumental) Warner Bros *WB 8018, 1970 (with The Faces)*

Reason To Believe/Maggie May
Mercury *6052 097, 1971*

Stay With Me/Debris Warner Bros *K 16136, 1971(with The Faces)*

Iko Iko/Mother Ain't Dead Warner Bros *K 16175, 1972 (with John Baldry - uncredited duet on B-side)*

You Wear It Well/Lost Paraguayos
Mercury *6052 171, 1972*

In A Broken Dream/Boogie Woogie Joe Youngblood *YB 1002, 1972 (with Python Lee Jackson - Rod featured on A-side only)*

Angel/What Made Milwaukee Famous
Mercury *6052 198, 1972*

Hi Ho Silver Lining/Rock My Plimsoul/Becks Bolero (instrumental) RAK *RR 3, 1972 (with Jeff Beck - Rod featured on B-side only)*

Cindy Incidentally/Skewiff (Mend The Fuse) Warner Bros *K 16247, 1973 (with The Faces)*

I've Been Drinking Again/Morning Dew/Greensleeves (instrumental) RAK *RR 4, 1973 (with Jeff Beck, vocal credited to Rod Stewart)*

Dishevelment Blues/Ooh La La Preview NME FLEXI, *1973 (with The Faces)*

Oh No Not My Baby/Jodie Mercury *6052 371, 1973 (B-side credits The Faces)*

Pool Hall Richard/I Wish It Would Rain (live) Warner Bros *K 16341, 1973 (with The Faces)*

Cindy Incidentally/Memphis/Stay With Me/Pool Hall Richard Warner Bros *K 16406, 1974 (with The Faces)*

Farewell/Bring It On Home - You Send Me Mercury *6167 033, 1974*

You Can Make Me Dance, Sing Or Anything/As Long As You Tell Him Warner Bros *K 16494, 1974 (credited to Rod Stewart/Faces)*

Am I Blue/Shine Penny Farthing *PEN 891, 1975 (with Ted Wood - Rod sings back-up vocals on B-side)*

Sailing/Stone Cold Sober Warner Bros *K 16600, 1975*

This Old Heart Of Mine/All In The Name of Rock 'n' Roll RIVA *1, 1975*

Skye Boat Song/Skye Boat Song (instrumental) RIVA *2, 1976 (with The Atlantic Crossing Drum & Pipe Band)*

It's All Over Now/Handbags And Gladrags Mercury *6167 327, 1976*

The Blues/Cloud Nine Youngblood *1077, 1976 (with Python Lee Jackson)*

Tonight's The Night/The Ball Trap
RIVA *3, 1976*

The Killing Of Georgie (Parts 1 & 2)/Fool For You RIVA *4, 1976*

Get Back/Trade Winds
RIVA *6, 1976*

Maggie May/You Wear It Well/Twistin' The Night Away Mercury *6160 006, 1976*

First Cut Is The Deepest/I Don't Want To Talk About It RIVA *7, 1977*

Memphis/You Can Make Me Dance, Sing Or Anything/Stay With Me/Cindy Incidentally RIVA *8, 1977 (with The Faces)*

Sailing/Stone Cold Sober
RIVA *9, 1977 (re-issue)*

Mandolin Wind/Sweet Little Rock'n'Roller/Girl From The North Country Mercury *6160 007, 1977*

You're In My Heart/You Got A Nerve
RIVA *11, 1977*

Hot Legs/I Was Only Joking
RIVA *10, 1978*

Ole Ola/I'd Walk A Million Miles - Que Sera Sera RIVA *15, 1978*

In A Broken Dream/If The World Stopped Still Old Gold *OG 9004, 1978 (with Python Lee Jackson - vocal on A-side only)*

Da Ya Think I'm Sexy/Dirty Weekend
RIVA *17, 1978*

Ain't Love A Bitch/Scared And Scarred
RIVA *18, 1979*

Blondes Have More Fun/The Best Days Of My Life RIVA *19, 1979*

If Loving You Is Wrong/Last Summer
RIVA *23, 1980*

Little Missunderstood/So Much To Say
Virgin *VS 366, 1980 (re-issue)*

Passion/Better Off Dead
RIVA *26, 1980*

Passion (extended version)/Better Off Dead RIVA *26T, 1980 (12")*

In A Broken Dream (stereo & mono versions)/The Blues/Cloud Nine Youngblood *YB EP89, 1980 (credited to Python Lee Jackson featuring Rod Stewart)*

In A Broken Dream/The Blues Youngblood *YB 1289, 1980 (12") (credited to Python Lee Jackson featuring Rod Stewart)*

My Girl/Somebody Special RIVA *28, 1980*

Oh God I Wish I Was Home Tonight/Somebody Special RIVA *29, 1981*

Tonight I'm Yours/Sonny RIVA *33, 1981*

Young Turks/Tora Tora Tora (Out With The Boys) RIVA *34, 1981*

How Long/Jealous RIVA *35, 1982*

Good Morning Little Schoolgirl/I'm Gonna Move To The Outskirts Of Town
Decca *F 11996, 1982 (re-issue)*

Baby Jane/Ready Now Warner Bros *W 9608, 1983*

Baby Jane/Ready Now/If Loving You Is Wrong (live) Warner Bros *W 96564T, 1983 (12")*

Little Missunderstood/So Much To Say
Immediate *IM 060, 1983 (re-issue)*

What Am I Gonna Do/Dancin' Alone
Warner Bros *W 9564, 1983*

What Am I Gonna Do/Dancin' Alone/Sailing (live) Warner Bros *W 9564T, 1983 (12")*

Sweet Surrender/Ghetto Blaster
Warner Bros *W 9440, 1983*

Sweet Surrender/Ghetto Blaster/Oh God I Wish I Was Home Tonight Warner Bros *W 9440T, 1983 (12")*

Sweet Surrender/Ghetto Blaster
Warner Bros *W 9440P, 1983 (7" picture disc)*

Infatuation/Three Time Loser
Warner Bros *W 9256, 1984*

Infatuation/Tonight's The Night/Three Time Loser Warner Bros *W 9256T, 1984 (12")*

Some Guys Have All The Luck/I Was Only Joking Warner Bros *W 9204, 1984*

Some Guys Have All The Luck/I Was Only Joking/The Killing of Georgie Warner Bros *W 9204T, 1984 (12")*

Trouble/Tora Tora Tora (Out With The Boys) Warner Bros *W 9115, 1984*

Trouble/This Old Heart Of Mine/Tora Tora Tora (Out With The Boys) Warner Bros *W 9115T, 1984 (12")*

People Get Ready/Back On The Street
Epic *A 6387, 1985*

People Get Ready/Back On The Street/You Know We Know
Epic *TA 6387, 1985 (12")*

Love Touch/Heart Is On The Line
Warner Bros *W 8668, 1986*

Love Touch/Heart Is On The Line/Hard Lesson to Learn
Warner Bros *W 8668T, 1986 (12")*

Love Touch/Heart Is On The Line/Hard Lesson To Learn Warner Bros *W 8668P, 1986 (12" picture disc)*

Every Beat Of My Heart/Trouble
Warner Bros *W 8652, 1986*

Every Beat Of My Heart (Tartan mix)/Trouble/Every Beat Of My Heart (LP version) Warner Bros *W 8625, 1986 (12")*

Every Beat Of My Heart (Tartan mix)/Trouble/Some Guys Have All The Luck (live)/I Don't Want To Talk About It (live) Warner Bros *W 8625TE, 1986 (limited edition 12")*

Maggie May/Reason To Believe
Mercury *CUT 20, 1986*

Another Heartache/You're In My Heart (live) Warner Bros *W 8631, 1986*

Another Heartache (extended version)/Another Heartache (edit)/You're In My Heart (live) Warner Bros *W 8631T (12") 1986*

In My Life/In My Own Crazy Way
Warner Bros *W 8489, 1986*

In My Life/In My Own Crazy Way/Tonight's The Night (live) Warner Bros *W 8489T, 1986 (12")*

In A Broken Dream/The Blues Bold Reprive Records *BRM 004, 1987*

In A Broken Dream (remix)/The Blues/Cloud Nine Bold Reprive Records *BRM 004T, 1987 (12")*

Twistin' The Night Away/Let's Get Small (instrumental)
Geffen *RODS 1, 1987*

Lost In You/Almost Illegal
Warner Bros *W 7927, 1988*

Lost In You (extended remix)/Lost In You (fade)/Almost Illegal
Warner Bros *W 7927T, 1988 (12")*

Lost In You (extended remix)/Lost In You (fade)/Almost Illegal
Warner Bros *W 7927TP, 1988 (12" picture disc)*

Maggie May/You Wear It Well
Old Gold *OG 9765, 1988*

Forever Young/Days Of Rage
Warner Bros *W 7796, 1988*

Forever Young (remix)/Days Of Rage/Forever Young (LP version)
Warner Bros *W 7796, 1988 (12")*

My Heart Can't Tell You No/The Wild Horse Warner Bros *W 7792, 1989*

My Heart Can't Tell You No/The Wild Horse/Passion (live) Warner Bros *W 7792T, 1989 (12")*

My Heart Can't Tell You No/The Wild Horse/Passion (live)
Warner Bros *W 7792TP, 1989 (12" picture disc)*

This Old Heart Of Mine/Ain't Love A Bitch Warner Bros *W 2686, 1989*

This Old Heart Of Mine/Ain't Love A Bitch/Tonight I'm Yours (Don't Hurt Me) Warner Bros *W 2686T, 1989 (12")*

This Old Heart Of Mine/Ain't Love A Bitch/Tonight I'm Yours Warner Bros *W 2686TP, 1989 (12" picture disc)*

Downtown Train/Stay With Me (with The Faces) Warner Bros *W 2647, 1989*

Downtown Train/Stay With Me (with The Faces)/Hot Legs
Warner Bros *W 2647, 1989 (12")*

Downtown Train/Stay With Me/Cindy Incidentally/To Love Somebody Warner Bros *W 2647TG, 1989 (limited edition 12")*

It Takes Two/Hot Legs Warner Bros *ROD 1, 1990 (with Tina Turner)*

It Takes Two (extended remix)/It Takes Two/Hot Legs (live) Warner Bros *ROD 1T, 1990 (12")*

It Takes Two (extended remix)/It Takes Two/Hot Legs (live) Warner Bros *ROD 1TP, 1990 (picture disc)*

Rhythm Of My Heart/Moment Of Glory Warner Bros *W00 17, 1991*

Rhythm Of My Heart/Moment Of Glory/I Don't Want To Talk About It (newly recorded) Warner Bros *W00 17T, 1991 (12")*

The Motown Song (re-mix)/Sweet Soul Music Warner Bros *W0030, 1991*

The Motown Song (re-mix)/Sweet Soul Music/Try A Little Tenderness Warner Bros *W0030TP, 1991 (12" picture disc)*

Broken Arrow/I Was Only Joking Warner Bros *W0059, 1991*

Broken Arrow/I Was Only Joking/The Killing Of Georgie Warner Bros *W0059TE, 1991 (10")*

My Town/The Tragedy Of Love EMI *EM 212, 1991 (with Glass Tiger, A side only)*

My Town/The Tragedy Of Love/Don't Forget Me (When I'm Gone) EMI *12EM 212, 1991 (with Glass Tiger, main title only) (12")*

People Get Ready/The Train Kept A'Rollin' Epic *657756 7. 1992 (with Jeff Beck, A-side only)*

Your Song/Broken Arrow Warner Bros *W0104, 1992*

Your Song/Broken Arrow/Mandolin Wind/The First Cut Is The Deepest Warner Bros *W0104T, 1992 (12")*

ORIGINAL ALBUMS

TRUTH
Shapes of Things/Let Me Love You/Morning Dew/You Shook Me/Ol' Man River/Greensleeves/Rock My Plimsoul/Beck's Bolero/Blues De Luxe/I Ain't Superstitious *Columbia SCX 6293, 1968 (with Jeff Beck)*

BECK OLA
All Shook Up/Spanish Boots/Girl From Mill Valley/Jailhouse Rock/Plynth (Water Down The Drain)/The Hangman's Knee/Rice Pudding *Columbia, SCX 6351, 1969 (with Jeff Beck)*

AN OLD RAINCOAT WON'T EVER LET YOU DOWN
Street Fighting Man/Man Of Constant Sorrow/Blind Prayer/Handbags And Gladrags/An Old Raincoat Won't Ever Let You Down/I Wouldn't Ever Change A Thing/Cindy's Lament/Dirty Old Town *Vertigo VO4, 1970*

FIRST STEP
Wicked Messenger/Devotion/Shake, Shudder, Shiver/Around The Plynth/Flying/Pineapple And The Monkey/Nobody Knows/Looking Out The Window/Three Button Hand Me Down *Warner Bros K 46053, 1970 (with The Faces)*

GASOLINE ALLEY
Gasoline Alley/It's All Over Now/Only A Hobo/My Way Of Giving/Country Comfort/Cut Across Shorty/Lady Day/Jo's Lament/I Don't Want To Discuss It *Vertigo 6360 500, 1970*

LONG PLAYER
Bad'n'Ruin/Tell Everyone/Sweet Lady Mary/Richmond/Maybel'm Amazed/Had Me A Real Good Time/On The Beach/I Feel So Good/Jerusalem. *Warner Bros K 46064, 1971 (with The Faces)*

EVERY PICTURE TELLS A STORY
Every Picture Tells A Story/Seems Like A Long Time/That's All Right/Amazing Grace/Tomorrow Is A Long Time/Henry/Maggie May/Mandolin Wind/(I Know) I'm Losing You/Reason To Believe *Mercury 6338 063, 1971*

A NOD'S AS GOOD AS A WINK
Miss Judy's Farm/You're So Rude/Love Lived Here/Last Orders Please/Stay With Me/Debris/Memphis/Too Bad/That's All You Need *Warner Bros K 56006, 1972 (with The Faces)*

NEVER A DULL MOMENT
True Blue/Lost Paraguayos/Mama You Been On My Mind/Italian Girls/Angel/Interludings/You Wear It Well/I'd Rather Go Blind/Twistin' The Night Away *Mercury 6499 163, 1972*

OOH LA LA
Silicone Grown/Cindy Incidentally/Flags And Banners/My Fault/Borstal Boys/Fly In The Ointment/If I'm On The Late Side/Glad And Sorry/Just Another Honkey/Ooh La La *Warner Bros K 56011, 1973 (with The Faces)*

COAST TO COAST/OVERTURES & BEGINNERS
It's All Over Now/Cut Across Shorty/Too Bad/Every Picture Tells A Story/Angel/ Stay With Me/I Wish It Would Rain/I'd Rather Go Blind/ Borstal Boy/Amazing Grace/Jealous Guy *Mercury 9100 001, 1974 (credited to Rod Stewart/Faces)*

SMILER
Sweet Little Rock'n'Roller/Lochinvar/Farewell/Sailor/Bring It On Home To Me You Send Me/Let Me Be Your Car/A Natural Man/Dixie Toot/Hard Road/I've Grown Accustomed To Her Face/Girl From The North Country/ Mine For Me *Mercury 9104 001, 1974*

ATLANTIC CROSSING
Three Time Loser/Alright For An Hour/All In The Name Of Rock'n'Roll/Drift Away/Stone Cold Sober/I Don't Want To Talk About It/It's Not The Spotlight/This Old Heart Of Mine/Still Love You/Sailing *Warner Bros K 56151, 1975*

A NIGHT ON THE TOWN
The Balltrap/Pretty Flamingo/Big Bayou/The Wild Side Of Life/Trade Winds/Tonight's The Night/First Cut Is The Deepest/Fool For You/The Killing Of Georgie (Parts 1 & 2) *Riva RVLP1, 1976*

FOOTLOOSE AND FANCY FREE
Hot Legs/You're Insane/You're In My Heart/Born Loose/You Keep Me Hanging On/(If Loving You Is Wrong) I Don't Want To Be Right/You Got A Nerve/I Was Only Joking *Riva RVLP5, 1977*

BLONDES HAVE MORE FUN
Da Ya Think I'm Sexy?/Dirty Weekend/Ain't Love A Bitch/The Best Days of My Life/Is That The Thanks I Get/Attractive Female Wanted/Blondes Have More Fun/Last

Summer/Standing In The Shadows of Love/Scared And Scarred *Riva RVLP8, 1978*

FOOLISH BEHAVIOUR
Better Off Dead/Passion/Foolish Behaviour/So Soon We Change/Oh God I Wish I Was Home Tonight/Gi' Me Wings/My Girl/She Won't Dance With Me/Somebody Special/Say It Ain't True(Cassette version contains extra track: I Just Want To Make Love To You) *Riva RVLP11, 1980*

TONIGHT I'M YOURS
Tonight I'm Yours (Don't Hurt Me/How Long/Tora Tora Tora (Out With The Boys)/Tear It Up/Only A Boy/Just Like A Woman/Jealous/Sonny/Young Turks/Never Give Up On A Dream *Riva RVLP14, 1981*

ABSOLUTELY LIVE
Tonight I'm Yours (Don't Hurt Me)/Sweet Little Rock'n' Roller/Hot Legs/Tonight's The Night/The Great Pretender/Passion/ She Won't Dance With Me/Little Queenie/You're In My Heart/Rock My Plimsoul/Young Turks/Guess I'll Always Love You/ Gasoline Alley/Maggie May/ Tear It Up/Da Ya Think I'm Sexy?/ Sailing/I Don't Want To Talk About It/Stay With Me *Riva RVLP17, 1982 (double LP)*

BODY WISHES
Dancin' Alone/Baby Jane/Move Me/Body Wishes/Sweet Surrender/What Am I Gonna Do (I'm So In Love With You)/Ghetto Blaster/Ready Now/ Strangers Again/Satisfied *Warner Bros 92 38771, 1983*

CAMOUFLAGE
Infatuation/Alright Now/Some Guys Have All The Luck/Can We Still Be Friends/Bad For You/Heart Is On The Line/ Camouflage/Trouble *Warner Bros 92 50951, 1984*

EVERY BEAT OF MY HEART
From Here To Eternity/Another Heartache/A Night Like This/Who's Gonna Take Me Home/Red Hot In Black/ Love Touch/In My Own Crazy Way/Every Beat Of My Heart/Ten Days Of Rain/In My Life *Warner Bros WX 53, 1986*

OUT OF ORDER
Lost In You/The Wild Horse/Lethal Dose Of Love/Forever Young/My Heart Can't Tell You No/Dynamite/Nobody Wants You When You're Down And Out/Crazy About Her/Try A Little Tenderness/When I Was Your Man *Warner Bros WX 152, 1988*

VAGABOND HEART
Rhythm Of My Heart/Rebel Heart/Broken Arrow/It Takes Two/ When A Man's In Love/You Are Everything/The Motown Song/Go Out Dancing/No Holding Back/Have I Told You Lately/Moment Of Glory/Downtown Train/If Only *Warner Bros WX 408, 1991*

ALBUM PRODUCTION WORK & GUEST APPEARANCES

PERMANENT DAMAGE - The GTOs Straight *STS 1059, 1969* Shock Treatment

IN A BROKEN DREAM - Python Lee Jackson *Youngblood SYB3001, 1969* In A Broken Dream/Cloud Nine/The Blues

IT AIN'T EASY - John Baldry *Warner Bros K 46088, 1971* Rod produced Side one. The album also features John Baldry's version of Flying.

EVERYTHING STOPS FOR TEA - John Baldry *Warner Bros K 46160, 1972* Rod produced one side and also sings a duet with Baldry on Mother Ain't Dead.

TOMMY - Various Artists *Ode SP 99001, 1972 (double LP)* Pinball Wizard

READING FESTIVAL - Various Artists *GM GML 1008, 1973* (I Know) I'm Losing You (live)

SCOTLAND SCOTLAND - Various Artists *Polydor 2383 282, 1974* Angel (duet with Dennis Law)

I'VE GOT MY OWN ALBUM TO DO - Ron Wood *Warner Bros K 56065, 1974* Mystifies Me/Take A Look At The Guy/If You Gotta Make A Fool Of Somebody (duets with Wood)

ALL THIS AND WORLD WAR II - Various Artists *Riva RVLP2 (double)* Get Back

THE MUSIC FOR THE UNICEF CONCERT - Various Artists *Polydor 2335 214, 1979* Da Ya Think I'm Sexy? (live)

1234 - Ron Wood *CBS 85227, 1981* Produced one track: Priceless

NIGHT SHIFT - Various Artists *Warner Bros K 57024, 1982* That's What Friends Are For

FLASH - Jeff Beck *Epic EPC 26112, 1985* People Get Ready

THE PRINCE'S TRUST - Various Artists *A&M AMA 3906, 1986* Sailing (live)

INNERSPACE - Various Artists *Geffen GEF 460223, 1987* Twistin' The Night Away

TWO ROOMS - Various Artists *Mercury 845 749-1, 1991* Your Song

SIMPLE MISSION - Glass Tiger *EMI 064-7 929221, 1991* My Town (duet with Alan Frew)

COMPILATIONS

SING IT AGAIN ROD
Reason To Believe/You Wear It Well/Mandolin Wind/Country Comfort/Maggie May/Handbags And Gladrags/Street Fighting Man/Twistin' The Night Away/Lost Paraguayos/(I Know) I'm Losing You/Pinball Wizard/Gasoline Alley *Mercury 6338 153, 1972*

THE VINTAGE YEARS 69-70
Repackaged coupling of Rod's first two albums: An Old Raincoat Won't Ever Let You Down & Gasoline Alley. *MERCURY 6672 013, 1976)/Double*

RECORDED HIGHLIGHTS & ACTION REPLAYS
Cut Across Shorty/Blind Prayer/Only A Hobo/Oh No Not My Baby/What Made Milwaukee Famous/An Old Raincoat Won't Ever Let You Down/Angel/ Cindy's Lament/Lady Day/Jo's Lament/ My Way Of Giving/It's All Over Now *Philips SON 001, 1976*

THE BEST OF ROD STEWART
Maggie May/Cut Across Shorty/An Old Raincoat Won't Ever Let You Down/(I Know) I'm Losing You/Handbags & Gladrags/It's All Over Now/Street Fighting Man/Gasoline Alley/Every Picture Tells A

Story/What Made Milwaukee Famous/Oh No Not My Baby/Jodie/You Wear It Well/Let Me Be Your Car/Pinball Wizard/Sailor/Angel/ Mine For Me *Mercury 6643 030, 1976/Double*

THE BEST OF ROD STEWART VOLUME II
Man Of Constant Sorrow/Blind Prayer/Lady Day/Tomorrow Is A Long Time/Country Comfort/Mandolin Wind/That's All Right/My Way Of Giving/I Don't Want To Discuss It/Reason To Believe/Italian Girls/I'd Rather Go Blind/Lost Paraguayos/True Blue/Sweet Little Rock'n'Roller/Hard Road/A Natural Man/Bring It On Home To Me - You Send Me/Twistin' The Night Away *Mercury 6619 031, 1977/Double*

THE BEST OF THE FACES
Flying/Around The Plynth/Nobody Knows/Three Button Hand Me Down/Sweet Lady Mary/Maybe I'm Amazed/Had Me A Real Good Time/Miss Judy's Farm/Memphis/Too Bad/Stay With Me/That's All You Need/Cindy Incidentally/Ooh La La/Flags And Banners/Borstal Boys/I Wish It Would Rain/Pool Hall Richard/You Can Make Me Dance, Sing Or Anything/It's All Over Now *RIVA RVLP3, 1977)/Double (with The Faces)*

THE FIRST SUPERGROUP
Back At The Chicken Shack/The In Crowd/Baby Take Me/Can I Get A Witness/Baby Baby/Holy Smoke/Cry Me A River/Oh Baby, Don't You Do It/Lord Remember Me *Charley 300020, 1977 (with The Steam Packet)*

A REASON TO BELIEVE
Maggie May/Reason To Believe/You Wear It Well/Lost Paraguayos/What Made Milwaukee Famous/Every Picture Tells A Story/Oh No Not My Baby/Bring It On Home To Me - You Send Me/An Old Raincoat Won't Ever Let You Down/Gasoline Alley/Sailor/Let Me Be Your Car *St Michael 21020102, 1978*

ROD STEWART GREATEST HITS VOL 1
Hot Legs/Maggie May/Da Ya Think I'm Sexy?/You're In My Heart/Sailing/I Don't Want To Talk About It/Tonight's The Night/The Killing Of Georgie/The First Cut Is The Deepest/I Was Only Joking *Riva ROD TV1, 1979*

THE FACES FEATURING ROD STEWART
Cindy Incidentally/On The Beach/Glad And Sorry/Maybe I'm Amazed/Shake, Shudder, Shiver/I Feel So Good/If I'm On The Late Side/Three Button Hand Me Down/Ooh La La/Looking Out The Window/Devotion/Had Me A Real Good Time *Pickwick SSP 3074, 1980 (with The Faces)*

HOT RODS
Let Me Be Your Car/Lost Paraguayos/Twistin' The Night Away/Mandolin Wind/Street Fighting Man/You Wear It Well/Sailor/Italian Girls/Pinball Wizard/Mine For Me/Jodie/Maggie May *Mercury 6463 061, 1980*

MAGGIE MAY
Maggie May/Sweet Little Rock 'n' Roller/Reason To Believe/Oh No Not My Baby/Sailor/Mandolin Wind/Twistin' The Night Away/Man Of Constant Sorrow/Street Fighting Man/Girl Of The North Country/Angel/It's All Over Now *Pickwick CN 2045, 1981*

ROD STEWART
You Wear It Well/Gasoline Alley/(I Know) I'm Losing You/Pinball Wizard/Every Picture Tells A Story/Amazing Grace/I'd Rather Go

Blind/I Don't Want To Discuss It/That's All Right/An Old Raincoat Won't Ever Let You Down/What Made Milwaukee Famous/Handbags And Gladrags *Pickwick CN 2059, 1982*

THE SHOTGUN EXPRESS
I Could Feel The Whole World Turn Round Underneath Me/Curtains/Funny 'Cos Neither Could I/Indian Thing (with The Shotgun Express) *See For Miles CYM 2, 1983, 10"*

THE HITS OF ROD STEWART
Maggie May/Gasoline Alley/Reason To Believe/Sailor/What Made Milwaukee Famous/You Wear It Well/Angel/Farewell/Handbags And Gladrags *Pickwick CN 2077, 1985*

THE BEST OF JEFF BECK
Shapes Of Things/Morning Dew/You Shook Me/I Ain't Superstitious/All Shook Up/Jailhouse Rock/Plynth/Hi Ho Silver Lining/Tallyman/Love Is Blue/I've Been Drinking/Rock My Plimsoul/Beck's Bolero/Rice Pudding *RAK FA 4131 251, 1985 (with Jeff Beck)*

THE ROCK ALBUM
Maggie May/You Wear It Well/Every Picture Tells A Story/(I Know) I'm Losing You/An Old Raincoat Won't Ever Let You Down/Lost Paraguayos/Twistin' The Night Away/Sweet Little Rock'n'Roller/Sailor/Let Me Be Your Car/That's All Right/Hard Road/Stay With Me (LIVE VERSION)/It's All Over Now (live) *Mercury 830 784-1, 1989*

THE BALLAD ALBUM
Reason To Believe/Mandolin Wind/I'd Rather Go Blind/Angel/Bring It On Home To Me - You Send Me/A Natural Man/Girl From The North Country/Mine For Me/Handbags And Gladrags/Country Comfort/Tomorrow Is A Long Time/Seems Like A Long Time/Jealous Guy (live)/I Wish It Would Rain (live) *Mercury 830 785-1, 1989*

BEST OF
Maggie May/Baby Jane/Da Ya Think I'm Sexy?/This Old Heart Of Mine/Sailing/I Don't Want To Talk About It/You're In My Heart/Young Turks/First Cut Is The Deepest/Tonight's The Night/Every Beat Of My Heart/Downtown Train *Warner Bros WX 314, 1989*

STORYTELLER
Good Morning Little Schoolgirl/Can I Get A Witness?/Shake/So Much To Say/Little Missunderstood/I've Been Drinking/I Ain't Superstitious/Shapes Of Things/In A Broken Dream/Street Fighting Man/Handbags And Gladrags/Gasoline Alley/Cut Across Shorty/Country Comforts/It's All Over Now/Sweet Lady Mary/Had Me A Real Good Time/Maggie May/Mandolin Wind/(I Know) I'm Losing You/Reason To Believe/Every Picture Tells A Story/Stay With Me/True Blue/Angel/ You Wear it Well/I'd Rather Go Blind/Twistin' The Night Away/What Made Milwaukee Famous/Oh No Not My Baby/Pinball Wizard/Sweet Little Rock 'n' Roller/Let Me Be Your Car/You Can Make Me Dance, Sing Or Anything/Sailing/I Don't Want To Talk About It/Stone Cold Sober/To Love Somebody/Tonight's The Night/The First Cut Is The Deepest/The Killing Of Georgie (Parts I & II)/Get Back/Hot Legs/I Was Only Joking/You're In My Heart/Da Ya Think I'm Sexy?/Passion/Oh God, I Wish I Was Home Tonight/Tonight I'm Yours/Young Turks/Baby Jane/What Am I Gonna Do (I'm So In Love With You)/People Get Ready/Some Guys Have All The Luck/Infatuation/Love Touch/Every Beat Of My Heart/Lost In You/My Heart Can't Tell You

No/Dynamite/ Crazy About Her/Forever Young/I Don't Want To Talk About It/This Old Heart Of Mine/Downtown Train *Warner Bros 9259871, 1989 (6 LP boxed set)*

THE ORIGINAL FACE
I Just Got Some/Bright Lights Big City/Ain't That Lovin' You Baby/Moppers Blues/Why Does It Go On/Shake/Keep Your Hands Off Her/Don't You Tell Nobody/Just Like I Treat You/Day Will Come/Just A Little Missunderstood/Baby Come Home/Sparky Rides/Can I Get A Witness/Baby Take Me *Thunderbolt THBL 085, 1990*

COMPACT DISC SINGLES

Lost In You (Fade)/Almost Illegal/Lost In You (Extended Remix)/Baby Jane *Warner Bros W 7927CD, 1988*

Forever Young (LP)/Days Of Rage/Forever Young (Remix)/Every Beat Of My Heart (LP) *Warner Bros W 7796CD, 1988*

My Heart Can't Tell You No/The Wild Horse/Passion (Live) *Warner Bros W 7729CD, 1989*

This Old Heart Of Mine/Ain't Love A Bitch/Tonight I'm Yours (Don't Hurt Me) *Warner Bros W 2686CD, 1989*

Downtown Train/Stay With Me (with The Faces)/Hot Legs *Warner Bros W 2647CD, 1989*

It Takes Two (Extended Remix)/It Takes Two/Hot Legs (Live) *Warner Bros ROD1CD, 1990 (with Tina Turner)*

Rhythm Of My Heart/Moment Of Glory/I Don't Want To Talk About It (Newly Recorded) *Warner Bros W 0017CD, 1991*

The Motown Song (Remix)/Sweet Soul Music (Live)/Try A Little Tenderness *Warner Bros W 0030CD, 1991*

Broken Arrow/I Was Only Joking/The Killing Of Georgie *Warner Bros W0059CD, 1991*

My Town/The Tragedy Of Love/Don't Forget Me (When I'm Gone)/Diamond Sun *EMI CDEM 212, 1991(with Glass Tiger, main title only)*

People Get Ready/'Cause We're Ended As`Lovers/Where Were You? *Epic 657756 2. 1992 (with Jeff Beck, main title only)*

People Get Ready/New Ways/Train Train/The Train Kept A Rolling *Epic 657756 5. 1992 (with Jeff Beck, main title only)*

Your Song/Broken Arrow/Mandolin Wind/The First Cut Is The Deepest *Warner Bros W0104CD, 1992*

ORIGINAL ALBUMS ON COMPACT DISC

Tracks same as LP's except where stated

FIRST STEP
Edsel ED CD 240, 1991

THE ROD STEWART ALBUM
Mercury 830 572-2, 1987

GASOLINE ALLEY
Mercury 824 881-2 M-1, 1984

EVERY PICTURE TELLS A STORY
Mercury 822 385-2 M-1, 1984

NEVER A DULL MOMENT
Mercury 826 263-2, 1987

SMILER
Mercury 832 056-2, 1987

ATLANTIC CROSSING
Warner Bros 256151, 1985

FOOTLOOSE & FANCY FREE
Warner Bros 927 323-2, 1990

BODY WISHES
Warner Bros 9 23877-2, 1983

CAMOUFLAGE
Warner Bros 9 25095-2, 1984

EVERY BEAT OF MY HEART
Warner Bros 925 446-2, 1986

OUT OF ORDER
Warner Bros 925 684-2, 1988
Contains extra track: Almost Illegal.

VAGABOND HEART
Warner Bros 7599-26598-2, 1991

GUEST APPEARANCES & PRODUCTION WORK ON CD

PERMANENT DAMAGE - The GTOs
Straight 7 73397-2, 1990

EVERYTHING STOPS FOR TEA - Long John Baldry *1991*

TOMMY - Various
ODE SP 88 001, 1972

THE PRINCE'S TRUST - Various
A&M CDA 3906, 1986

CANCEL EVERYTHING - Ronnie Wood
Thunderbolt CDTB 2.034, 1987

FLASH - Jeff Beck *Epic CDEPC 26112, 1985*

TWO ROOMS - Various *Mercury 845 7491, 1991*

SIMPLE MISSION - Glass Tiger
EMI 7 929222, 1991 My Town (duet with Alan Frew)

COMPILATIONS ON COMPACT DISC

GREATEST HITS
Warner Bros 256744, 1982 Track listing same as LP

SING IT AGAIN ROD
Mercury 824 882-2 M-1, 1984 Track listing same as LP

THE LATE SIXTIES WITH ROD STEWART
Hi Ho Silver Lining/Tallyman/Love Is Blue/Beck's Bolero/Rock My Plimsoul/ I've Been Drinking Again/Shapes Of Things/Let Me Love You/Morning Dew/You Shook Me/All Shook Up/Spanish Boots/Jailhouse Rock/Plynth (Water Down The Drain)/ Hangman's Knee/Rice Pudding/Ol' Man River/ Greensleeves/I Ain't Superstitious (with Jeff Beck) *EMI, CZ130, 1988 (CD only)*

THE ROCK ALBUM
Mercury 830 784-2, 1989 Track listing same as LP

THE BALLAD ALBUM
Mercury 830 785-2, 1989 Track listing same as LP

IN A BROKEN DREAM
In A Broken Dream/The Blues/Cloud Nine/Sparky Rides/Red Ballroom/Why Does It Go On/The Day Will Come/I Just Got Some/Shake/Bright Lights Big City/Keep Your Hands Off Her/ Ain't That Loving You Baby/Don't You Tell Nobody/Moppers' Blues/Just Like I Treat You *CRC ROCK, 3021 2, 1989* (CD only)

BEST OF
Warner Bros 926 034-2, 1989 Contains four extra tracks to LP version: You Wear It Well/I Was Only Joking/ What Am I Gonna Do/The Killing Of Georgie

STORYTELLER
Warner Bros. 925 987-2, 1989 (4 CD) Track listing same as LP

MAGGIE MAY
Pickwick PWKS 586, 1990 Track listing same as LP

THE ORIGINAL FACE
Thunderbolt CDTB 085, 1990 Track listing same as LP

IN A BROKEN DREAM
In A Broken Dream/The Blues/Cloud Nine/Sparky Rides/Red Balloon/Why Does It Go On/The Day Will Come/Keep Your Hands Off Her/Just A Little Missunderstood/I Just Got Some/ Shake/Bright Lights Big City/Ain't That Loving You Baby/Don't You Tell Nobody/Moppers' Blues/Just Like I Treat You *Success 2195CD, 1990* (CD only)

AIN'T THAT LOVIN' YOU BABY
Why Does It Go On/I Just Got Some/Shake/Bright Lights Big City/Just A Little Missunderstood/Keep Your Hands Off Her/Ain't That Loving You Baby/Don't Tell Nobody/Moppers' Blues/Just Like I Treat You/Sparky Rides/Red Ball Room *ONN 75, 1990* (CD only)

GASOLINE ALLEY/SMILER
Mercury 846 988-2, 1991

TRUTH/BECK OLA
EMI CDP 7954692, 1991 Coupling of the two Jeff Beck albums on one CD.

BRING IT BACK HOME
You Wear it Well/Handbags And Gladrags/Street Fight/Mine For Me/Hard Road/Amazing Grace/I'd Rather Go Blind/Farewell/ Bring It On Home - You Send Me/North Country/ Dirty Old Town/ Let Me Be Your Car/Italian Girls/True Blue/ Sailor/ Tomorrow Is Such A Long Time *Pickwick PWKS 4091 P, 1991* (CD only)

The following bona fide Rod Stewart albums were not yet available on CD in the UK at the time this discography was compiled, although they are widely available on import:

LONG PLAYER
Warner Bros WPCP-4037 1990: Japan

A NOD'S AS GOOD AS A WINK
Warner Bros WPCP-4038 1990: Japan

OOH LA LA
Warner Bros WPCP-4039, 1990: Japan

A NIGHT ON THE TOWN
Warner Bros 3116-2, 1988: US

BLONDES HAVE MORE FUN
Warner Bros 3261-2, 1988: US

FOOLISH BEHAVIOUR
Warner Bros 18P2-2979, 1989: Japan

TONIGHT I'M YOURS
Warner Bros. 3602-2, 1988: USA

ABSOLUTELY LIVE
Warner Bros. 9 23743-2, 1989: USA

IMPORTANT OVERSEAS RELEASES

Maybe I'm Amazed (Studio Version)/Rear Wheel Skid
Warner Bros 16078, 1971: France A-side not released in UK (7")

Killing Of Georgie/Rosie
Warner Bros WBS 8396, 1977: US B-side not released in UK (7")

Da Ya Think I'm Sexy? (Remix)/Scared And Scarred *Warner Bros WBSD 8727, 1978: US (12") A-side not released in UK*

Crazy About Her/Dynamite *Warner Bros 7-27657, 1989: US A-side different mix to album version (7")*

Crazy About Her (Just A Crazy Sure Mix)/Crazy About Her (B! Crazy Dub)/Crazy About Her (Kyle Wild West Edit)/Crazy About Her (Acca Dub)/Dynamite
Warner Bros 0-21268, 1989: US (12") Four different mixes none of which was released in the UK

Crazy About Her (Kyle Wild West Edit)/Crazy About Her/(Just A Crazy Sure Mix)/Crazy About Her (instrumental) *Warner Bros PRO, USA (Promotional CD single, instrumental unavailable elsewhere)*

The Motown Song (single remix), The Motown Song (power mix), *Warner Bros PRO, USA (Promotional CD single, power mix unavailable elsewhere)*

BOOKS

THE ROD STEWART STORY - *George Tremlett (Futura, 1976)*

ROD STEWART & THE CHANGING FACES - John Pidgeon *(Panther, 1976)*

ROD STEWART - Richard Cromelin *(Sire-Chappell, 1976)*

A LIFE ON THE TOWN - Peter Burton *(New English Library, 1977)*

ROD STEWART - Tony Jasper *(Octopus, 1977)*

ROD STEWART - Paul Nelson & Lester Bangs *(Sidgwick & Jackson, 1982)*

ROD STEWART - Jurgen Seibold *(Moewig, 1991) Germany*

ROD STEWART - A BIOGRAPHY - Tim Ewbank & Stafford Hildred *(Headline, 1991)*

FANZINES

FOOLISH BEHAVIOUR
Issues 1- 4, 1983-1984. Photocopied magazine run by the now defunct Rod Stewart & Faces Friends Club.

SMILER
Issues 1 - 32, 1981 - 1992. Glossy high quality colour/B&W quarterly. Available from The Official Rod Stewart Fan Club, P.O. Box 241, Telford, Shropshire, U.K. and PO Box 66043, Unicity Postal Outlet, Winnipeg, Manitoba R3K 2E7, Canada.

VIDEOS

ROD STEWART LIVE AT THE LA FORUM
Hot Legs/Tonight's The Night/Da Ya Think I'm Sexy?/I Just Wanna Make Love To You/Blondes Have More Fun/(If Loving You Is Wrong) I Don't Want To Be Right/Wild Side Of Life/You're In My Heart/Sweet Little Rock'n'Roller/Stay With Me/Twistin' The Night Away *Warner Home Video, 1981*

TONIGHT HE'S YOURS
Gi' Me Wings/Sweet Little Rock'n'Roller/Tear It Up/Passion/ Dance With Me - Little Queenie/You're In My Heart/Rock My Plimsoul/Get Back/Hot Legs/Young Turks/(If Loving You Is Wrong) I Don't Want To Be Right/Tora Tora Tora (Out With The Boys)/Gasoline Alley/Maggie May/Da Ya Think I'm Sexy?/I Was Only Joking/You Wear It Well/Wild Side Of Life *Embassy, 1982*

THE ROD STEWART CONCERT VIDEO
Infatuation/Bad For You/Tonight's The Night/I Don't Want To Talk About It/Dance With Me/Hot Legs/You're In My Heart/Baby Jane/Sittin' On The Dock Of The Bay/Young Turks/Passion/Da Ya Think I'm Sexy?/Maggie May/Some Guys Have All The Luck/Stay With Me/We'll Meet Again. *(Karl Lorimar, 1986) USA only.*

ROD STEWART & THE FACES VIDEO BIOGRAPHY 1969-1974
Three Button Hand Me Down/It's All Over Now/Gasoline Alley/(I Know) I'm Losing You/I Feel So Good/Memphis Tennessee/Stay With Me/Miss Judy's Farm/Memphis/That's All You Need/I'd Rather Go Blind/You Wear It Well/Angel/Cindy Incidentally/Pool Hall Richard/Sweet Little Rock'n'Roller/You Can Make Me Dance, Sing Or Anything *Video Collection, 1988*

ROD STEWART VIDEOS 1984 -1991
Infatuation/Some Guys Have All The Luck/People Get Ready/Every Beat Of My Heart/Lost In You/Forever Young/ My Heart Can't Tell You No/This Old Heart Of Mine/Downtown Train/It Takes Two/Rhythm Of My Heart/The Motown Song/Broken Arrow *Warner Music Vision, 1991*

PROMOTIONAL VIDEOS

Oh No Not My Baby *(1973)* Farewell *(1974)* Bring It On Home To Me/You Send Me *(1974)* Sailing *(1975)* Tonight's The Night *(1976)* First Cut Is The Deepest *(1976)* You're In My Heart *(1977)* Hot Legs *(1977)* I Was Only Joking *(1977)* You're Insane *(1977)* Da Ya Think I'm Sexy *(1978)* Ain't Love A Bitch *(1978)* Blondes Have More Fun *(1978)* Passion *(1980)* Dance With Me *(1980)* Oh God I Wish I Was Home Tonight *(1980)* Tonight I'm Yours *(1981)* Young Turks *(1981)* How Long *(1981)* Just Like A Woman *(1981)* Baby Jane *(1983)* What Am I Gonna Do? *(1983)* Infatuation *(1984)* Some Guys Have All The Luck *(1984)* Alright Now *(1984)* Love Touch *(1986)* Every Beat Of My Heart *(1986)* Another Heartache *(1986)* Twistin' The Night Away *(1987)* Lost In You *(1988)* Forever Young *(1988)* My Heart Can't Tell You No *(1988)* Crazy About Her *(1989)* This Old Heart Of Mine *(1989)* Downtown Train *(1989)* It Takes Two *(1990)* Rhythm Of My Heart *(1991)* The Motown Song *(1991)* Broken Arrow *(1991)*

SELECTED COMPACT DISC BOOTLEGS

REAL GOOD TIME
(I Know)I'm Losing You/Bring It On Home To Me/Sweet Little Rock'n'Roller/Fly In The Ointment/Every Picture Tells A Story/Stay With Me/Motherless Children/Gasoline Alley/You Wear It Well/Maggie May/ Twistin' The Night Away *Swingin Pig TSP-CD-039, 1989*

THAT'S ALL YOU NEED
Miss Judy's Farm/Too Bad/That's All You Need/True Blue/Twistin' The Night Away/I Don't Wanna Discuss It/Cut Across Shorty/ Bad'n'Ruin/It's All Over Now/Had Me A Real Good Time/I'm Losing You *Oh Boy 1-9035, 1990*

KILLER HIGHLIGHTS 1972 - 1973
Had Me A Real Good Time/Maybe I'm Amazed/Love In Vain/Jealous Guy/Cut Across Shorty/Bad'n'Ruin/It's All Over Now/Memphis/If I'm On The Late Side/My Fault/Stealer/Borstal Boys/Too Bad/I'm Losing You *Scorpio F90-8072, 1990*

PLYNTH
World Production 1090 D 060-2, 1990 Same track listing as album version

ROD STEWART LIVE IN FRANKFURT 1980
Hot Legs/Born Loose/Tonight's The Night/She Won't Dance With Me/You're In My Heart/I Don't Wanna Be Right/Passion/Sweet Little Rock'n'Roller *Super Golden Radio Shows SGRS 036, 1991*

FOREVER YOUNG
Hot Legs/Lost In You/Sweet Little Rock'n'Roller/Dock Of The Bay/Sweet Soul Music/First Cut Is The Deepest/ Forever Young/Twistin' The Night Away/Da Ya Think I'm Sexy?/Every Picture Tells A Story/Reason To Believe - You Wear It Well - Maggie May - You're In My Heart/Try A Little Tenderness *Rock Solid RS 006/007, 1991 (double)*

ONLY THE LUCKY ONE
Maggie May/Rhythm Of My Heart/Sweet Little Rock'n'Roller/Downtown Train/Hot Legs/Some Guys Have All The Luck/Tonight's The Night/Da Ya Think I'm Sexy/Time To Time/Every Beat Of My Heart/First Cut Is The Deepest/If Only/Reason To Believe/Baby Jane/ Passion/I Don't Want To Talk About It/Twistin' The Night Away/ Sailing (duet with Chris De Burgh) *Red Phanton RPCD 2058/2059, 1991 (double)*

THE STORY SO FAR
Disc 1 - The Faces: It's All Over Now/Cut Across Shorty/Too Bad/Every Picture Tells A Story/Angel/Stay With Me/I Wish It Would Rain/(I Know) I'm Losing

You/Jealous Guy (live in Anaheim, November 1973)/Stay With Me (live in New York, 1973)/Bring It On Home To Me - You Send Me/Sweet Little Rock'n'Roller/Fly In The Ointment/ Motherless Children/Gasoline Alley/ Maggie May/Twistin' the Night Away *(live in Detroit, 1974)*

Disc 2 - You Wear It Well/Tonight's The Night/Maggie May (live in Newcastle, 1977)/Hot Legs/Da Ya Think I'm Sexy/You're In My Heart (live in Manchester, 1978)/Hot Legs/Tonight's The Night/Maggie May/You're In My Heart/Get Back/You Wear It Well/Passion/I Was Only Joking/Stay With Me *(live at Wembley, 1980)*

Disc 3 *Tribute to Otis, all recorded live in the USA, 1990:* Intro/Hot Legs/Lost In You/Sweet Little Rock'n'Roller/ Sitting On the Dock Of The Bay/Sweet Soul Music/Try A Little Tenderness/First Cut Is The Deepest/Forever Young/Twistin' The Night Away/Da Ya Think I'm Sexy/ Every Picture Tells A Story/Reason To Believe/You Wear It Well/Maggie May/You're In My Heart. *Beach Martin Records BM 039/3, 1991 (triple)*

SELECTED BOOTLEGS

THE PERFORMANCE
Three Button Hand Me Down/Maybe I'm Amazed/Country Comfort/Love In Vain/Medley: Had Me A Real Good Time, Every Picture Tells A Story/ Medley: Plynth, Did You Ever, Gasoline Alley, Never Knew What It Was
Ruthless Rhymes Ltd, 1971

DANCING IN THE STREETS
Losing You/Turn Me On/Dancing In The Streets/Love In Vain/Maybe I'm Amazed/Because I'm Used To Her/ Country Comfort *1972*

THE BEST OF ROD STEWART & THE SMALL FACES
Same track listing as 'Dancing In The Streets' *1972*

HAD ME A REAL GOOD TIME
You're My Girl/Cut Across Shorty/Love In Vain/Bad'n'Ruin/ It's All Over Now/Had Me A Real Good Time/Losing You *Trademark Of Quality, 1972*

PLYNTH
Wicked Messenger/Flying/Too Much Loving For A Hen-Pecked Man/Love In Vain/I Don't Wanna Discuss It/Country Comfort/Plynth/Honky Tonk Women/ Gasoline Alley/It's All Over Now *Trademark Of Quality, 1972*

AFTER HOURS
(I Know) I'm Losing You/Bring It On Home To Me - You Send Me/Sweet Little Rock'n'Roller/Fly In The Ointment/Too Bad - Every Picture Tells A Story/Stay With Me/Motherless Children/Gasoline Alley/Maggie May/Twistin' The Night Away *TKRWN 1811, 1975*

EUROPEAN TOUR 1976
Three Time Loser/You Wear It Well/Big Bayou/Tonight's The Night/Wild Side Of Life/Maggie May/Angel/You Keep Me Hanging On/True Blue *1977*

RHYTHM & BOOZE
Three Time Loser/You Wear It Well/Tonight's The Night/Maggie May/Angel/You Keep Me Hanging On/I'm Losing You/Twistin' The Night Away/You're In My Heart *Ruthless Rhymes Ltd, 1978*

A LOT FOR NOTHING
Hot Legs/Tonight's The Night/Get Back/I Don't Want to Talk About It/Sweet Little Rock'n'Roller/Da Ya Think I'm Sexy/ Sailing/Twistin' The Night Away/You Wear It Well/Maggie May *1979*

Year	Title	UK PEAK	US PEAK
1971	Reason To Believe/Maggie May	1	1
1972	I Know I'm Losing You	NR	24
1972	Stay With Me (with The Faces)	6	17
1972	Handbags And Gladrags	NR	42
1972	You Wear It Well	1	13
1972	In A Broken Dream *(with Python Lee Jackson)*	3	56
1972	Angel/What Made Milwaukee Famous	4	40
1973	Cindy Incidentally *(with The Faces)*	2	48
1973	Twistin' the Night Away	NR	59
1973	I've Been Drinking Again *(with Jeff Beck)*	27	NR
1973	Oh No Not My Baby	6	59
1973	Pool Hall Richard	8	NR
1974	Farewell	7	NR
1974	Mine For Me	NR	91
1974	You Can Make Me Dance *(with The Faces)*	12	-
1975	Sailing	1	58
1975	This Old Heart Of Mine	4	83
1976	Tonight's The Night	5	1
1976	The Killing Of Georgie	2	30
1976	Sailing (re-entry)	3	-
1976	Get Back	11	NR
1976	Maggie May (EP)	31	NR
1977	First Cut Is The Deepest/I Don't Want To Talk About It	1	22/46
1977	The Faces EP *(with The Faces)*	41	NR
1977	You're In My Heart	3	4
1978	Hot Legs/I Was Only Joking	5	22/28
1978	Ole Ola	4	NR
1978	Da Ya Think I'm Sexy	1	1
1979	Ain't Love A Bitch	11	22
1979	Blondes Have More Fun	63	NR
1980	If Loving You Is Wrong	23	NR
1980	Passion	17	5
1981	My Girl	32	NR
1981	Somebody Special	NR	71
1981	Tonight I'm Yours	8	20
1982	Young Turks	11	5
1982	How Long	41	49
1983	Baby Jane	1	14
1983	What Am I Gonna Do	3	38
1983	Sweet Surrender	23	NR
1984	Infatuation	27	6
1984	Some Guys Have All The Luck	15	10
1984	Alright Now	NR	72
1985	People Get Ready	-	48
1986	Love Touch	27	6
1986	Every Beat Of My Heart	2	53
1986	Love Touch (re-entry)	69	-

Year	Title	UK PEAK	US PEAK
1986	Another Heartache	54	52
1987	Sailing (2nd re-entry)	41	-
1987	Twistin' The Night Away	-	80
1988	Lost In You	21	12
1988	Forever Young	57	12
1989	My Heart Can't Tell You No	49	4
1989	This Old Heart Of Mine	51	10
1990	Downtown Train	10	3
1990	It Takes Two *(with Tina Turner)*	5	NR
1991	Rhythm Of My Heart	3	5
1991	The Motown Song	10	10
1991	Broken Arrow	54	20
1991	My Town *(uncredited backing vocals Glass Tiger)*	34	NR
1992	People Get Ready (re-issue) *(with Jeff Beck)*	49	NR
1992	Your Song/Broken Arrow	48*	NR

ALBUMS

Year	Title	UK PEAK	US PEAK
1968	Truth	-	15
1969	Cos Nostra Beck Ola	39	15
1969	An Old Raincoat	-	139
1970	First Step	45	119
1970	Gasoline Alley	62	27
1971	Long Player	31	29
1971	Every Picture Tells A Story	1	1
1971	A Nod's As Good As A Wink	2	6
1972	Never A Dull Moment	1	2
1973	Ooh La La	1	21
1973	Sing It Again Rod	1	31
1974	Coast To Coast (live)	3	63
1974	Smiler	1	13
1975	Atlantic Crossing	1	9
1976	A Night On The Town	1	2
1976	Best Of	18	90
1977	Best Of The Faces	24	NR
1977	Footloose And Fancy Free	3	2
1978	Blondes Have More Fun	3	1
1979	Greatest Hits	1	22
1980	Foolish Behaviour	4	12
1981	Tonight I'm Yours	8	11
1982	Absolutely Live (live)	35	46
1983	Body Wishes	5	30
1984	Camouflage	8	18
1986	Every Beat Of My Heart	5	28
1988	Out Of Order	11	20
1989	Storyteller	-	54
1989	Best Of	3	NR
1990	Downtown Train	NR	20
1991	Vagabond Heart	2	10

* Still on chart and rising at time of publication
(NR = Not Released)
Source: Music Week (UK) & Billboard (US)